BEFORE INDIA

EXPLORING YOUR
ANCESTRY WITH DNA

DAVID G. MAHAL

Published by DGM Associates
PO Box 1146
Pacific Palisades, CA 90272

ISBN-13: 978-0692218204
ISBN-10: 0692218203

Library of Congress Control Number: 2014910916
DGM Associates, Pacific Palisades, CA

Printed by CreateSpace, an Amazon.com Company
North Charleston, SC

Printed in the United States of America

Available from Amazon.com and other retail outlets
Available on Kindle and other devices

DEDICATION

To my parents and ancestors.

CONTENTS

INTRODUCTION

"In all of us there is a hunger, marrow-deep, to know our heritage—to know who we are and where we have come from."—Alex Haley

Alex Haley, a black American writer, is best known as the author of *Roots: The Saga of an American Family*.[1] His book is based on his family's history, starting with the story of Kunta Kinte, who was kidnapped in Gambia in 1767 and transported to the United States to be sold as a slave. Haley claimed to be a seventh-generation descendant of Kunta Kinte.

The book *Roots* was published in thirty-seven languages and Haley won a special award in 1977 from the Pulitzer Board. The book was adapted into a popular television miniseries by the American Broadcasting Corporation. It won several prestigious awards, with its finale standing as the third-highest-rated US television program ever.

Later, Haley attempted to trace his family history in another book. He was unable to fully prove his research by traditional genealogical methods using birth, marriage, and death certificates,

David G. Mahal

because his ancestors were African American slaves, and very little documentation about them was available. Because female slaves were often raped by their owners and produced children, there was usually no record of the true father, so Haley relied on oral histories handed down from generation to generation as his primary source of information. He was eventually able to trace his ancestry back to William Baugh, a Scottish overseer of a slave plantation in Alabama who was thought to have fathered a child with a black slave called Sabrina. Their son was thought to have been born between 1850 and 1860.

Recent DNA tests established that Haley was directly descended from a Scottish paternal bloodline. The findings came to light after a sample of DNA from Haley's black nephew matched that of his distant white cousin who lived in Wales and whose shared lineage started in seventeenth-century Scotland. The findings at the website ancestry.co.uk were the first scientific confirmation of Haley's research.

There are other interesting examples. According to the firm BritainsDNA, Prince William, the Duke of Cambridge, is likely to be between 0.3 and 0.8 percent Indian.[2] Apparently one of Prince William's maternal ancestors was the daughter of a Scottish trader with the East India Company and his Armenian-Indian housekeeper. Although researchers are not absolutely certain of their findings so far, a monarch of partial Indian descent may be the future king of Britain.

The study of family histories and lineages is known as genealogy (from the Greek *genea*, generation, and *logos*, knowledge). Genealogy records of many Indian families have been maintained by Brahman Pandits, also known as Pandas, in handwritten registers at the holy city of Haridwar in India. For some families, these records go back many centuries, but such records do not exist for most families in India because not everyone has followed this practice. This practice is not well known today for many Indians who settled abroad. However, these days there are literally hundreds of websites devoted to genealogy. Some Indians have started adding their records to databases maintained by commercial websites such as Ancestry.com and FamilyTreeDNA.com. So far there are not many such records, but this is likely to change in the future.

The pursuit of family history and origins is usually motivated by curiosity to know who our ancestors were, the need to see how we fit into the overall picture, and the need to preserve the past for future generations. My own family history has been passed down through oral recitations by elders and written records. Some members from the current generation tried to research and document whatever information they could collect. A few stories have been passed down such as the story that someone from the court of Akbar the Great, about five hundred years ago, wanted to marry and take away one of the Mahal girls he had seen. On learning about this possibility, the Mahal clan fled from where they lived at the time to a remote part of Punjab in North India. There are stories about members of the family who held positions in the court of Maharaja Ranjit Singh at the turn of the eighteenth century. The family tree is incomplete, although some branches go back about ten generations. The earliest name is from the year 1760. Sadly, the names of many other ancestors are lost forever.

Looking deeper into history, my grandfather wrote a book about the antiquity of the Jats, which is my ethnic group. Since his book was published in 1955,[3] historians and academics have published more books about the Jats. The conclusion in practically all these books is similar: the Jat people are descendants of Medes or Scythians who arrived and lived in a large part of northern India at one time. Some historians have claimed that Jats are descendants of Aryans. The evidence tends to be anecdotal such as the similarity of certain words of the language, comparisons of some habits and social customs, and what others have written. Historical discrepancies remain regarding when these people arrived and whether they were peaceful or violent. Most writers have said more or less the same thing in different words. Considering the great diversity of people in India and the differences in physiognomy among our community, I have always been skeptical about the Jats being descendants of any single group of people.

Aroused by my own curiosity, a few years ago I participated in the Genographic Project at the National Geographic Society and had my DNA analyzed to explore my ancestry in more definite terms.[4] The results were amazing. They showed that my ancestry could be traced thousands of years before any groups like the Medes or Scythians arrived in India and that many people in India other than the Jats also shared my genetic background. This knowledge led me to study the science of DNA analysis and explore the ancestral issues related to a much larger number of ethnic groups in India.

In his book about the antiquity of Jats, my grandfather wrote, "This brief work is meant chiefly to excite the ambition of interested research worker ..." I think he would approve of the approach I took, using scientific and other knowledge that did not exist during his time. I have arranged this book in three parts.

PART ONE—SHAPING THE PAST

The book starts by clarifying that without robust verification, traditional methods of research about ancestry—building upon what others have written—tend to perpetuate misinterpretations and errors. In many instances, we end up drinking wine of the same vintage from different bottles, so to speak. No disrespect is intended toward scholars who have used this methodology to explain ancestry. It is understood that in studying ancestry, more reliable techniques such as DNA analysis were not available until

David G. Mahal

recently. As the book will show, based on current scientific knowledge it is time for historians and scientists to converge and start a dialogue.

PART TWO—POPULATING INDIA

The second part provides a brief review of the origin of our planet and how life evolved. The development of modern humans from primates is discussed along with where people originated and how they dispersed and populated this planet. This part of the book provides a summary of the diverse groups of people who came to India starting thousands of years ago and eventually populated the subcontinent. These incursions were both peaceful and violent. The migrants intermixed with local populations, and as a result, India today is a colorful tapestry of hundreds of ethnic groups with distinct cultures and languages. The ancestry of these people goes to many corners of this planet. This section explains how different marital arrangements influence a family's pedigree tree and shows that our pool of ancestors is very large and complex.

PART THREE—DNA SCIENCE

The third part covers the science of genes and genealogy. It describes the Human Genome Project (HGP) that surveyed the genetic design of the human being. This project was completed in 2000. There are explanations about what genes are and how DNA analysis is used to more accurately trace ancestry. DNA testing is a relatively new technology for genealogists, and it allows them to trace paternal or maternal lines.

This part includes my study of the DNA results of 1,291 individuals in fifty-two key ethnic communities from the Indian subcontinent (including some ethnic communities in Bangladesh, Malaysia, Pakistan, Singapore, Sri Lanka, and the United Kingdom) to determine their origins. The results of the study identified eight major ancestral groups for this population. The conclusion is that these ethnic communities do not have pure ancestral lines. They tend to have several ancestral lines, and in most cases, the lineages are shared with other ethnic communities. In spite of their differences in culture, language, and religion, many members of these communities are related in the past.

Although some chapters of this book are applicable to people everywhere, it is mostly about ancestors who came to the Indian subcontinent long before it was known by its current name. The book concludes with suggestions about how readers can have their DNA tested and explore their deep ancestry more precisely.

David G. Mahal
Los Angeles, California
October 2014

PART ONE
SHAPING THE PAST

A s General George Patton once said, "If everybody is thinking alike, then somebody isn't thinking." Traditional methods of historical research about ancestry—reading and building upon what someone else has already written—tend to perpetuate misinterpretations and historical errors wherever they may exist. As shown later in this book, there are several recent scientific developments about ancestry that provide much better answers.

CHAPTER 1

CREATING HISTORY

"History will be kind to me, for I intend to write it."—Winston Churchill

History is not something waiting to be discovered. It is the story we tell about our past. There is no history that we can reflect upon until it is recited or written by someone, so the quality or accuracy of history depends on the conduits: the reciters and writers.

People often let their experiences filter the way they interpret the past. For this reason, it is important that those seeking to study the work of another devote some effort to the study of that person. Only then can a student of history effectively judge the work in its proper light. What was the author's motivation? Was the author trying to make a personal point? Was the author, like Winston Churchill, trying to project his or her own life and experiences in a positive light? Dan Brown, author of *The Da Vinci Code*, aptly said, "By its very nature, history is always a one-sided account."[1]

David G. Mahal

LANGUAGE ISSUES

There are two major avenues to better understand the ancient world: archaeology and written texts. Although archaeologists have excavated objects that are millions of years old, there are no written records of ancient history. Written language happens to be a recent development.

It is appropriate to review how language developed for humans. Chimpanzees use distinct warning calls for different predators, and gorillas use sign language, so the capability for communicating predates the evolution of modern humans. Most scholars assume that full language ability in humans evolved by about one hundred thousand years ago. By this time, humans had developed a larger skull with the brain functions and a vocal tract to articulate a variety of sounds. This enabled them to link vocal sounds with meaning, and language evolved.

1.1 - Mesopotamian Tablet

Most languages were spoken for a long time

12

but not written. Some of the earliest written records are the pictures and symbols carved on shells and stones in various parts of the world. Eventually these pictures and symbols appeared on clay tablets. Numbers were written long before letters and words.

It is generally agreed that the earliest written language was invented in Mesopotamia (Sumer, present Iraq) around 3200 BCE. The cuneiform system of writing that developed went beyond the use of pictograms.

The earliest form of Sanskrit, known as Vedic Sanskrit, goes back to about 1700 BCE. The Tamil language in South India has a literature going back to about the same time. The Indian scholar Panini formulated the Sanskrit grammar in the fourth century BCE, and Chinese and Greek were first written about 1500 BCE. The Albanian language, spoken north of Greece, was not written down until about the same time.

Humans developed writing systems and created scripts that write from left to right, right to left, and vertically. But the written records go back only a few thousand years in human history.

DOCUMENTING HISTORY

The Romans and Greeks were the first to take a formal interest in writing down history (from the Greek *historia*, "knowledge gained from inquiry"). One of the first recorded dates for a historical event was 648 BCE, when the poet Archilochus witnessed an eclipse of the sun and noted it in a poem. There is no comprehensive written account of Indian history before this time period.

Historians started documenting what they saw and heard only during the last 2500 years or so, but what they write cannot always be relied upon. In many instances, what they write represents the unverified accounts of others. They have a tendency to contradict each other. For instance, about the death of Attila the Hun, one historian wrote, "he died of a nosebleed by suffocating on his own blood."[2] An account of Attila's death by the Roman chronicler Count Marcellinus reported, "Attila, King of the Huns and ravager of the provinces of Europe, was pierced by the hand and blade of his wife."[3] There are similar contradictions in other writings.

Long before Alexander the Great's invasion of India in 327 BCE, the Greeks possessed fragments of information about India but not from reading Indian texts or visiting India. Most of what the Greeks knew of India came by word of mouth from soldiers, merchants, and officials in the Persian Empire. Some of the earliest writers of Indian history include Herodotus, Ptolemy (there are two of them), Megasthenes, Strabo, Ktesias (or Ctesias), and Pliny. Megasthenes is the only one who spent considerable time in India and made observations of his own.

HERODOTUS

Let us consider Herodotus, a Greek historian, who is used as a source of information in several books and writings about ancient India. Many Indian historians have relied considerably on what he wrote. He was a storyteller who lived from 484–425 BCE in modern day Turkey. He produced one lengthy book, *The Histories*, which has been translated and divided into nine volumes. There are several different editions of this book. For Herodotus, history meant "inquiry," and his writings are devoted not only to the past but also to geography, ethnology, and myth.

Herodotus made his living from lecturing, and his readings found audiences, especially in Athens. He seems to have traveled extensively around the Mediterranean, conducting interviews and collecting stories for his book. There is no evidence that he visited India, although a few writings say so. It is unclear how reliable his sources were and whether he validated what he heard with other sources.

1.2 - Herodotus

15

David G. Mahal

Scholars of his time had different opinions about him. Cicero called Herodotus the "father of history,"[4] yet the Greek writer Plutarch, in his *Moralia* (Ethics), dubbed Herodotus the "father of lies."[5] Plutarch suggested that Herodotus's appeal lay in his flattering accounts of Greek exploits and accused him of deliberate falsehood. Herodotus's reputation as a liar did not end with Plutarch. Many other critics accused him of passing on the stories of his informants as history. Because of the strange narrations and the folktales he documented, a few of which are described in the following pages, several other critics also branded him the "father of lies."

Some scholars argued that Herodotus exaggerated the extent of his travels and invented his sources.[6] Even Alexander the Great was aware that Herodotus's fanciful accounts of India were based on hearsay.[7] Vincent Smith, one of the earliest Indian historians, wrote nearly one hundred years ago about "hearsay notes [regarding India] recorded by the Greek author Herodotus."[8]

The *Imperial Gazetteer of India* declared more than one hundred years ago that Herodotus's "accounts of India are among the oldest records of Indian civilization by an outsider."[9] That may be the case, but it does not mean that the information presented was reliable. Some examples of Herodotus's views regarding India are provided below as translated from his work, *The Histories* (the book references denote the volume in which the writing appears).[10]

About the Callatiae People of India

In Book 3.38, Herodotus says,

> "When he [Darius] was king of Persia, he summoned the Greeks who happened to be present at his court, and asked them what they would take to eat the dead bodies of their fathers. They replied that they would not do it for any money in the world. Later, in the presence of the Greeks, and through an interpreter, so that they could understand what was said, he asked some Indians, of the tribe called Callatiae, who do in fact eat their parents dead bodies, what they would take to burn them. They uttered a cry of horror and forbade him to mention such a dreadful thing."

About the Padaei People of India

In Book 3.99, he says,

> "There are many tribes of Indians, speaking different languages, some pastoral and nomadic, others not ... Another tribe further to the east is nomadic, known as the Padaei; they live on raw meat. Among their customs, it is said that when a man falls sick, his closest companions kill him, because, as they put it, their meat would be spoiled if he were allowed to waste away with disease. The invalid, in these circumstances, protests that there is nothing the

17

David G. Mahal

matter with him – but to no purpose. His friends refuse to accept his protestations, kill him and hold a banquet."

He continues in Book 3.99,

"Should the sufferer be a woman, her women friends deal with her in the same way. If anyone is lucky enough to live to an advanced age, he is offered in sacrifice before the banquet – this, however, rarely happens, because most of them will have had some disease or other before they get old, and will consequently have been killed by their friends."

Apparently the Callatiae and Padaei were small, primitive tribes that may have been necrophagous (they ate corpses). There is considerable archeological and anthropological evidence to suggest that some prehistoric humans practiced cannibalism in Africa, the Amazon rainforest, the Middle East and Far East, Australia, and New Zealand. The practice lingered into recent times in some parts of Africa, Fiji, and Indonesian New Guinea.[11]

It is not clear exactly where the Callatiae and Padaei lived. Contrary to the apparent funerary cannibalism practiced by these tribes, there are enough archaeological excavations to show that even several thousand years before Herodotus's time, Indians buried their dead in the Indus Valley. As an example, Mohenjo

Daro is a major settlement of the Indus civilization. The name means "mound of the dead," and it contains many burial sites.

About Black Semen

In Book 3.101, Herodotus says,

> "All the Indian tribes I have mentioned copulate in the open like cattle; their skins are all of the same colour, much like the Ethiopians'. Their semen is not white like other peoples', but black like their own skins; the same is to be found in the Ethiopians. Their country is long way from Persia towards the south, and they were never subject to Darius."

(Note: There is some confusion about geography. India is eastward of Persia, not southward.)

A search on the medical website *mayoclinic.org* indicates that dark semen may be caused by mixing it with blood; the condition, known as hematospermia, is an infection and/or inflammatory condition of the male prostate. Such medical conditions were probably unknown in the fifth century BCE. Nevertheless, it seems preposterous for Herodotus to attribute such a condition to a country's entire male population without questioning the source and investigating the matter more thoroughly.

David G. Mahal

About Giant Ants

In Book 3.102, he continues,

> "There is found in this desert a kind of ant of great size –
> bigger than a fox, though not so big as a dog ... These
> creatures as they burrow underground throw up the sand
> in heaps ... The sand has rich content of gold, and this is
> what the Indians are after when they make their
> expeditions into the desert ... When the Indians reach the
> place where the gold is, they fill the bags they have brought
> with them with sand, and start for home again as fast as
> they can go; for the ants (as is said in the Persian story)
> smell them and at once give chase; nothing in the world
> can touch these ants for speed, so not one of the Indians
> would get home alive, if they did not make sure of a good
> start while the ants were mustering their forces."

French ethnologist Michel Peissel discovered an animal species
that may explain the giant ants Herodotus wrote about. Peissel
says that in an isolated region of northern Pakistan, formerly India,
there exists a species of marmot, which is a type of burrowing
squirrel. The Minaro tribal people he interviewed confirmed that
for generations, they have collected the gold dust that the marmots
bring to the surface when they are digging burrows.[12]

What Herodotus heard was likely a "tall tale" the local tribes told to frighten outsiders from seeking the gold dust. He also wrote that specimens of these giant ants were caught and brought back to Persia.

About Lions

In Book 3.108, he writes,

> "A lioness, on the contrary, the most bold and powerful of the beasts, produces but a single cub, once in her life – for she expels from her body not only the cub, but her womb as well – or what is left of it. The reason for this is that when the unborn cub begins to stir, he scratches at the walls of the womb with his claws, which are sharper than any other animal's, and as he grows bigger scrabbles his way further and further through them until, by the time he is about to be born, the womb is almost wholly destroyed."

As people familiar with animals know, this is incorrect. A lioness can have up to six cubs, usually every two years. As with many other animals, the claws of the cub are soft before birth and do not harm the uterus.

HISTORICAL INACCURACIES

By 500 BCE, the Achaemenid Persian Empire founded by Cyrus the Great stretched from the Indus Valley (Harappa, Mohenjo

David G. Mahal

Daro, and Taxila) in the east to Thrace and Macedon on the northeastern border of Greece. It is believed that Herodotus wrote his accounts around 440 BCE. In depicting the Indians as savages, it is obvious that he was ignorant of the highly developed civilization that existed in India before and during his time. The following historical events had taken place or were occurring across the border of the Persian Empire:

• **Based on archaeological findings,** Mehrgarh, the precursor to the Indus Valley Civilization, was established in northern India about 6,500 years before Herodotus's writings.

• Apparently Herodotus was unaware of the Indus Valley Civilization that existed in northern India until about one thousand years before his time.

• Indo-European speakers, called Aryans by some historians, migrated into India long before Herodotus's writings.

• The earliest hymns of the Rig Veda were composed in northern India about five hundred to one thousand years before Herodotus's writings.

• Mahavira (599–527 BCE) established the central tenets of Jainism in India many years before Herodotus's writings.

•   Gautama Buddha (563–483 BCE) established the central tenets of Buddhism in India before Herodotus's writings.

•   By about 700 BCE, long before the universities of Oxford, Cambridge, and Bologna were established, the world's first major center of higher learning was founded in Taxila, with students from all parts of India and some adjoining countries.[13] Although Darius the Great annexed Taxila to the Achaemenid Persian Empire around 500 BCE, apparently Herodotus was unaware of this seat of higher learning across the border.

These examples are noteworthy, because many Indian and other historians seem to be in awe about Herodotus and base their conclusions on his writings. Indeed, archaeology has begun to prove that many things in *The Histories,* his major book, are largely accurate. Much of the information that he provided about his times is extremely valuable, primarily because there is not much else available. But it is also safe to conclude that he was ignorant about India, and the few bizarre stories he wrote impart no credibility to his writings about this part of the world. While his work should be valued, many of the tales he wrote about India, and possibly about some other parts of the world that he never visited, are myths that have no place in history.

THUCYDIDES

Not all the historians of Herodotus's time used the same style of

David G. Mahal

gathering and disseminating information. Thucydides (460–400 BCE) has been called the "father of scientific history" because of his strict standards of evidence gathering and analysis. He chronicled nearly thirty years of war between Athens and Sparta. His *History of the Peloponnesian War* sets a standard for accuracy that makes it a defining text, as he relied on the testimony of eyewitnesses and his experiences as a general during the war.[14] He did not write anything about India.

KTESIAS

Ktesias (or Ctesias, born 416 BCE) was a Greek doctor who wrote several books about Persia and a treatise about India called the *Indika*. Unfortunately, most of his work has been lost. His writings were largely based on oral reports of Persian officials and others who visited India.

His accounts describe some of the aboriginal tribes that existed in the land. He wrote about people who were short, like pygmies, and a tribe that barked like dogs.[15] He wrote about people in certain Indian valleys who lived for two hundred years and had white hair in their youth that turned black when they grew old.[16] It is unknown who kept records of such longevity. More importantly, why were the secrets of such longevity not remembered or recorded? There are reports of people with the heads of dogs and of men and women with tails, eight fingers on each hand and as many toes on each foot, and ears that covered their shoulders. There are tales of a race of people with no neck and eyes that rested in their shoulders. It is possible that people with remarkable deformities existed at that time, but it is also possible that many of these stories were based on local superstitions and mythologies that the Greeks interpreted as truths.[17] As in the case of Herodotus, these are unverified stories. If we use a strict historical tradition, the unsupported and fragmentary nature of these writings renders them unreliable.

PTOLEMY I SOTER

Ptolemy, a Macedonian nobleman (367–283 BCE), was one of the successor kings to the empire of Alexander the Great. He traveled with Alexander in Egypt and India, served as one of his trusted bodyguards, and became the king of Egypt, declaring himself King Ptolemy I (later Soter, for "savior").

Although a senior member of the army, Ptolemy I was also a historian and wrote a biography of Alexander. His accounts of India are sparse, because

1.3 - Ptolemy I Soter

David G. Mahal

Alexander's army stayed around the Indus River and did not go very far into India.

MEGASTHENES

Along with Ptolemy I, Seleucus I also succeeded Alexander the Great. He set up the Seleucid dynasty that extended to the Indus River in northwest India. Megasthenes (350–290 BCE) became the Greek ambassador of Seleucus I to the court of Chandragupta Maurya in Pataliputra (present-day Patna). He was probably the first foreign ambassador in India.

He was a traveler and geographer to whom the subsequent Greek writers were indebted for their accounts of India. He is said to have lived in India for many years and visited South India and Sri Lanka as well. His firsthand reports about the culture, history, and religion became the basis of Western knowledge about India.

STRABO

Born to an affluent family in what is now Turkey, Strabo (64/63 BCE to CE 24) was of Greek ethnicity, and he traveled extensively but did not visit India. He wrote a series of books titled *Geography*, and in one of these books, he described India based on accounts he had heard. In sharp contrast to other historians, he carefully qualified the source of his information. The historian A. V.

Williams Jackson provides a translation of Strabo's opening comments:

> "The reader must receive this account of India with indulgence, for the country lies at a very great distance, and few persons of our nation have seen it; and those who have visited it have seen only some portions of it; the greater part of what they relate is from hearsay, and even what they saw, they observed during their passage through the country with an army, and in great haste. For this reason they do not agree in their accounts of the same things, although they write about them as if they had examined them with the greatest care and attention."[18]

PLINY THE ELDER

Pliny the Elder (CE 23–79), a Roman scientist, naturalist, and author, was killed when Mount Vesuvius erupted and destroyed Pompeii and Herculaneum in one of the most catastrophic events in European history. He is credited with compiling *The Natural History*, an encyclopedic work divided into thirty seven books.

Pliny provided detailed descriptions of voyages taken by others including one from Alexandria to South India, up the Nile to Coptos, through the desert to Berenice at the Red Sea, and across the Indian Ocean to the port of Muziris near Kochi (Cochin).

David G. Mahal

His writings contain interesting facts such as Rome's expenditure of gold for its trade with India and the sale of imported Indian products at one hundred times the original price.

He also wrote about the existence of large sea creatures in the Indian Ocean, piracy on the seas, and some people of the Indian subcontinent with bizarre physical deformities.

1.4 - Pliny the Elder

CLAUDIUS PTOLEMY

Claudius Ptolemaeus, a Greco-Egyptian scientist and scholar, also known as Ptolemy (a common name in those times; not to be confused with Ptolemy I Soter), lived from about CE 100–170. He is known for his extensive writings on astronomy, geometry, astrology, and geography.

He codified latitude and longitude and placed the grid system on the map. His treatise on geography consisted of eight volumes, the last of which was an atlas that included details about India. He had to rely on mariners for a lot of his information, which was not always accurate. Although a genius of his time, he wrongly proposed an Earth-centered Universe, with the Sun and planets revolving around the Earth. His concept was replaced with the proposal of a Sun-centered Universe by scholars like Copernicus, Nicholas de Casa, Ibn al-Shatir (Arab Islamic astronomer), and India's Aryabhata and Bhaskara. There are craters on the Moon and Mars named in his honor.

IN SHORT

1.5 - Claudius Ptolemaeus

Historians tend to quote each other, and the first person who writes something unique is referenced repeatedly by others. As Napoléon Bonaparte once remarked, "History is the version of past events that people have decided to agree upon."[19]

History tends to perpetuate, but the historian's primary responsibility is to provide reliable narratives. Since the nineteenth century, academics and historians have paid careful attention to how sources are chosen and interpreted.[20] This has not been the case with all earlier historians, even those of considerable repute. We need to be cautious about the accuracy of historical information, whether it has been verified, and how it is interpreted and used. We should also remember that written history goes back less than 2500 years.

David G. Mahal

Some historians have written about the ancestors of ethnic groups in India based on the works of these early writers, which were not always correct or verified. As Carl Sagan remarked, "Extraordinary claims require extraordinary evidence." In science, every hypothesis is tested and confirmed or rejected by others. In history this is not always the case. We cannot ignore history, but as we will see later in this book, when it comes to deep ancestry, scientific evidence provides more dependable answers.

PART TWO

POPULATING INDIA

This part of the book provides a brief review of the origin of our planet and how life evolved. The development of modern humans from primates is discussed along with where people originated and how they dispersed and populated this planet. There is a historical summary of the groups of people who came to India thousands of years ago and eventually populated the subcontinent. As a result, India today is a colorful tapestry of hundreds of unique ethnic groups with distinct cultures and languages.

CHAPTER 2

THE BEGINNINGS

"The most incomprehensible thing about the universe is that it is comprehensible."—Albert Einstein

Sri Prem Baba, a guru from Sao Paolo, Brazil, spends several months each year in Rishikesh, India. He says the following about his life as a child:

"I'd ask my mother, 'Who made the world?' She'd say it was God. And then I'd ask, 'Who made God?'"

"Don't think about it," his mother said, "or you'll go mad." [1]

Like Sri Prem Baba, we have all gazed at the stars and puzzled over how the universe was formed. We ask, "How did Earth begin? Where did people come from?" Our line of questioning always returns to the origin of things: how did it all start?

David G. Mahal

THE UNIVERSE

The nature of the universe is beyond ordinary human understanding. Looking at the sky at night we can observe the Milky Way galaxy which contains our solar system. This is a complex gravitationally bound system consisting of stars, planets, meteorites, gas, dust, and a veritable assortment of unknown dark matter astronomers have yet to see. This galaxy is thought to contain over one hundred billion stars and planets. Furthermore, our galaxy is just one of many in a vast universe. Photographs from the Hubble Space Telescope, which orbits about 350 miles (570 km) above the Earth, reveal thousands of galaxies in a single picture. It is estimated there are at least one hundred billion such galaxies in the observable universe. Some scientists have theorized that our universe is not the only one, and that many other universes exist parallel to each other. The James Webb Telescope, set to launch in 2018, will sit at an incredible distance of 930,000 miles (1.5 million km) from Earth. It will help us learn a lot more about the universe. As Carl Sagan explained very nicely, "… we float like a mote of dust in the morning sky [of this vast universe]."

Let us consider distances. Light moves at a velocity of 186,000 miles (300,000 kilometers) per second. On this basis, the distance light can travel in one year (called *light-year*) is 5,878,000 million miles (9,461,000 million kilometers). Alpha Centauri, the nearest star system to our solar system, is about 4.37 light-years away. The planet Kepler 186f, which is roughly the same size as Earth, is some 500 light-years away from Earth. That means its light we see now started traveling in our direction 500 years ago (think about the distance). In some cases, by the time we see a light from outer space its point of origin may no longer exist.

AGE OF THE UNIVERSE

The beginning of the universe has been a subject of religious, mythological, and scientific discussion for a long time. On the scientific side, Sir Isaac Newton guessed that the universe was a few thousand years old. Einstein, the developer of the general theory of relativity, preferred to believe that the universe was ageless and eternal. Jainism and Hinduism hold the same belief.

In the 1920s, Belgian mathematician and Catholic priest Georges Lemaitre described the beginning of the universe as a burst of fireworks spreading out in a growing sphere. The "big bang," a term coined in 1949 by Cambridge astrophysicist Fred Hoyle to explain the phenomenon, became the accepted scientific model of the development of the universe. According to this theory, the universe was in an extremely hot, dense state that exploded (creating the "big bang") and expanded rapidly. If it can be imagined, the universe was a single point at the moment of the explosion. The time of that moment has been estimated by measuring the rate of the expansion of the universe and extrapolating backward. This widely accepted theory presents the most comprehensive and accurate explanation so far.

The theory is based on two key studies. In 1929, Edwin Hubble, working with the one-hundred-inch telescope on Mount Wilson in Pasadena, California, discovered that all galaxies are moving away from us. This led him to the conclusion, which was later accepted by the scientific community, that the universe is expanding.[2]

In June 2001, a National Aeronautics and Space Administration (NASA) explorer mission, the Wilkinson Microwave Anisotropy Probe (WMAP), was launched to study the properties of the universe as a whole. How did this probe help determine the age of

**2.1 - WMAP Satellite
(Courtesy: NASA)**

the universe? Einstein's general theory of relativity was used to compute how fast the universe was expanding, and the clock was turned back to determine when the universe had "zero" size, according to Einstein. The time between then and the present was computed

36

as the age of the universe. Based on this model, the best current estimate of the age of the universe is 13.7 billion years with a 1 percent margin of error.[3]

Where did that single point, at the moment of creation when the universe had zero size, come from? Dr. Martin Bojowald and other physicists at Pennsylvania State University have explored the time before the "big bang" with a mathematical time machine called Loop Quantum Gravity. The theory combines equations of quantum physics that did not exist in Einstein's day. It is the first mathematical description to deduce properties of a universe before the "big bang," but it is not clear if this model is better at explaining the present.

AGE OF THE EARTH

How old is our Earth? This topic has also produced many discussions in classrooms, on television and radio, and in churches, colleges, and seminaries. There are two primary sides:

- The religious "young Earth" proponents believe in the biblical age of the Earth and the universe (about six thousand years).

- The scientific "old Earth" proponents believe in the scientific age of the Earth (several billion years).

David G. Mahal

The difference in these viewpoints is significant and requires a historical review to determine which one is more reasonable.

The "young Earth" view came from the Bible. Genesis 1 says that the Earth was created on the first day (Genesis 1:1–5). From there, the age of the Earth can be calculated by taking the first five days of creation (from Earth's creation to Adam), following the genealogies to Abraham, and adding the time from Abraham to today. The creation of Adam is depicted in a fresco on the Sistine Chapel in the Vatican that Michelangelo painted in 1511. It illustrates the biblical story from Genesis in which God breathed life into Adam.

If Adam was created on the sixth day after creation, there were five days before him. The time from Adam to the prophet Abraham is about two thousand years, and most scholars agree that Abraham lived about four thousand years ago. Therefore, the biblical age of the Earth and the universe is about six thousand years (5 days + 2,000 years + 4,000 years). In 1650, Archbishop James Ussher of Ireland published the exact date of creation as Sunday, October 23, 4004 BCE.

Most Eastern religions assert that the Earth is much older. According to the Hindu viewpoint, the Earth is involved in an eternal cycle of creation and destruction, and each cycle of time, called the "day of Brahma," is equal to about 4.32 billion years.[4] In

Jainism, the Earth is regarded as "eternal."[5] Aristotle also believed that the Earth existed eternally.

Regarding the "old Earth" view, scientists have not found a way to determine the exact age of the Earth from rocks, because the oldest rocks on Earth have been recycled and changed by nature. Nevertheless, scientists have dated an ancient crystal called a zircon to about 4.4 billion years. It is the oldest known piece of the Earth's crust and was found in 2001 in an area north of Perth in Australia.[6] Tests in 2008 on a pinkish tract of bedrock on the eastern shore of Canada's Hudson Bay showed its age to be 4.28 billion years.[7] Based on such scientific "old Earth" evidence, the current best estimate of the age of our planet is about 4.55 billion years.[8]

THE MYSTERY OF OUR ORIGINS

In 2005, NASA deliberately crashed the Deep Impact space probe into a comet called Tempel 1 that was hurtling through space. The dust stirred up on the surface of this comet was analyzed in NASA's Jet Propulsion Laboratory (JPL) in Pasadena, California, through the Spitzer telescope that drifts in an Earth-trailing orbit around the sun. The results revealed the presence of several chemicals: silicates, such as those found on beaches; carbonates, the minerals in seashells; carbon-containing compounds found in car exhaust and on burnt toast; iron-bearing compounds; a large amount of water, and other materials that are found on Earth. Scientists have discovered iso-propyl cyanide in a cloud 27,000 light-years from Earth, suggesting life-bearing chemistry in space.[9]

How such materials are formed in outer space and appear in comets and other objects like meteorites is beyond the scope of this book. It is sufficient to note that many chemicals and molecules that are essential for life have been falling to the Earth's surface from outer space for billions of years. Even now, about 670,000 pounds (300,000 kilograms) of organic material from comet dust and about 22 pounds (10 kilograms) of organic materials sealed inside meteorites land on Earth each year.[10] Did such materials from outer space create the first self-replicating biological molecule on Earth?

THE MIRACLE OF LIFE

Among the earliest evidence for life on Earth are discoveries of biogenic graphites in rocks in Western Greenland and microbial mat fossils in sandstone in Western Australia.[11] From microscopic organic beginnings about 3.5 billion years ago, life evolved into a variety of species that have flourished under the oceans and above. Many species adapted and survived, and many became extinct. There are many living species that we do not know much about. Consider the scarlet jellyfish, *Turritopsis dohrnii*, living in the ocean. It was discovered in 1988 by Christian Sommer, a young German student. This remarkable sea creature is considered "immortal." When it gets old or injured, it does not die; miraculously, it simply rejuvenates itself. Dr. Shin Kubota at Kyoto University in Japan has been studying the jellyfish and trying to learn its secrets.[12] Overall, there are about ten million species alive on our planet at this time, and a rich variety of fauna and flora exists.

THE SEARCH FOR ANSWERS

Launched in March 2004, by the European Space Agency (ESA), the unmanned spacecraft Rosetta took a long 10-year trek to reach the comet 67P/Churyumov/Gerasimenko, named "Chury" for short. It went into orbit around the comet on August 6, 2014.[13] At a distance of about 250 million miles (400 million kilometers), messages take over 22 minutes to travel between Rosetta and Earth.

2.2 - Computer model of Rosetta satellite (Courtesy: NASA)

David G. Mahal

Chury may be a piece of primordial, icy debris left over from the original formation of our solar system more than 4.55 billion years ago. It looks like a small peanut shaped icy body covered by cliffs, circular ridges and

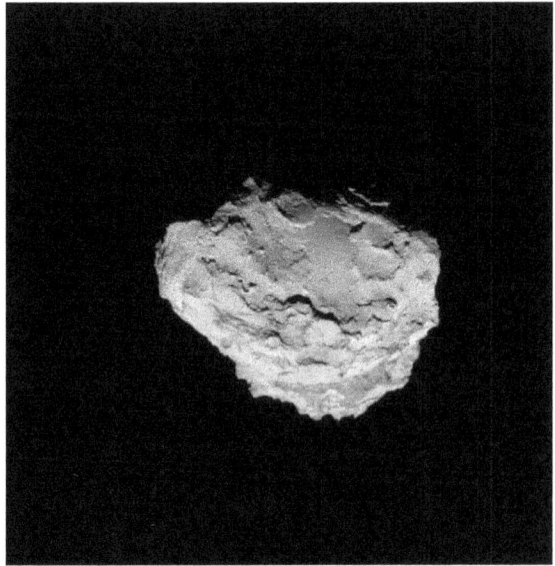

2.3 67P/Churyumov-Gerasimenko Comet
(Copyright: ESA/Rosetta/NAVCAM)

smooth plains. Later in 2014, after moving Rosetta closer to Chury, attempts will be made to place a lander named Philae on its surface to out carry out several experiments. Rosetta carries eleven unique scientific experiments, and Philie carries ten additional experiments.

There are many aspects of life on Earth that are not totally clear. For instance, the Earth's atmosphere has contained oxygen, necessary for life, for only the last 10 percent of our planet's history. The origin of water, also necessary for life, is not fully settled in the scientific community. The Rosetta mission will attempt to gain knowledge of comets and their role in possibly delivering water and the building blocks of life around the early solar system.

CHAPTER 3

HUMAN ORIGINS

"It is not the strongest or the most intelligent who will survive but those who can best manage change." — Charles Darwin

From the start of life on Earth, we need to skip forward a few billion years to the time of the primates or mammals from which humans emerged. The oldest known fossil of a primate was discovered in a lake bed in China's Hubei Province near the Yangtze River. Named Archicebus, the fossil is fifty-five million years old, and it represents a diminutive, long-tailed monkey that was about the size of a mouse.[1] The finding supports the theory that primates probably emerged in Asia and migrated to other parts of the world, including Africa, where some groups evolved into humans.

Physical and genetic similarities show that the modern human has a close relationship to another group of primates: the so-called great apes of Africa. Molecular evidence shows that the prehuman species split from our closest relative, the chimpanzee, five to six million years ago.

A relationship with other primates has been difficult to accept. In 1619, the Italian philosopher and freethinker Lucilio Vanini was burned alive for suggesting that humans evolved from apes. Two centuries later, popular society remained contemptuous. During the first half of the nineteenth century, the scientific community was closely tied to the church. When Charles Darwin published *On the Origin of Species* in

3.1 - Hominid

1859, many Europeans were deeply disturbed. On hearing about the theory of human evolution, the wife of an Anglican bishop is said to have exclaimed, "Descended from the apes? My dear, we will hope it is not true, but if it is, let us pray that it may not become generally known." To her disappointment, it did not remain a secret.

KEY FOSSIL EVIDENCE

Paleontology is the study of what fossils tell us about the past and about our evolution. The early history of mankind is based on archaeological finds. Unearthed fragments of ancient fossils provide the only clues to our ancient past, and sometimes a few bones are all we have to tell us about species that lived thousands or millions of years ago. These fossils enable researchers to study changes in body size, locomotion, brain, diet, and other aspects regarding the way of life for early humans. Stone tools, figurines, paintings, footprints, and other records tell us where and how early humans lived.

From what paleontologists have discovered, the earliest humans evolved in Africa, and much of human evolution occurred on that continent. The fossils of early humans and prehuman species or hominids (ancestors with a more upright posture) that lived between two and six million years ago come mostly from Africa.

3.2 - Ramapithecus

Like the rest of our planet, the Indian subcontinent has been full of life for millions of years. Archaeological remains have been found in different parts of India to reconstruct the history of this

David G. Mahal

early period. The remains of the prehuman species *Sivapithecus* and *Ramapithecus*, which existed from eight to fourteen million years ago, were found in the Shivalik hills of Punjab in North India and later discovered in Africa and Saudi Arabia.

Remains and replicas of apes and ancient mammals, such as giant elephants and turtles, from several million years ago are displayed in the Shivalik Fossil Park near Chandigarh. Fossils of gazelles, rhinoceroses, crocodiles, giraffes, and rodents that are up to fourteen million years old are on display at the Pakistan Museum of Natural History in Islamabad.

3.3 - Giant Elephants, Shivalik Fossil Park

During the 1930's, German paleoanthropologist Ralph von Koenigswald found a large fossil primate molar that belonged to the largest known apes that ever lived, standing up to 9.8 feet (3 meters), and weighing up to 1,190 lbs. (540 kg). He named the species *Gigantopithecus bilaspurensis*, which lived 6 to 9 million years ago in India, and *Gigantopithecus blacki*, which lived in China until at least 1 million years ago.

3.4 - Giant Turtles, Shivalik Fossil Park

THE MILLENNIUM MAN

In December 2000, the discovery of fossilized remains of an early ancestor was announced in Kenya by a team of scientists from the College de France in Paris and the Community Museums of Kenya. The fossil was named *Orrorin tugenensis* ("original man in the Tugen region"), otherwise known as the Millennium Man. It is estimated to be at least six million years old.[2] Since then, distinct body parts belonging to at least five other individuals, both male and female, have been unearthed in the same area. The specimens are about the size of a chimpanzee. They could climb trees and had bipedal (walking) abilities.

47

David G. Mahal

ARDI

In 1994, a fossil of a human ancestor named *Ardipithecus ramidus* (*ramid* means "root" in the Afar language of Ethiopia and refers to the connection of this fossil to humanity) or "Ardi" was found in Ethiopia by a team led by anthropologist Tim White from the University of California, Berkeley. Ardi lived about 4.4 million years ago and had both tree-climbing and bipedal abilities. About one hundred other fossils of this type have been found.

3.5 - Lucy

LUCY

The skeleton of *Australopithecus afarensis* ("southern ape of the Afar region") was found by American paleoanthropologist Donald Johanson and his colleagues in Ethiopia in 1974.[3] The fossil was nicknamed "Lucy" after the Beatles' song "Lucy in the Sky with Diamonds," which was popular at that time. Lucy lived about 3.2 million years ago, was less than four feet tall, and had a brain about one-third the size of the modern human brain. About three hundred other fossils like Lucy have been found. The species had both tree-climbing and bipedal abilities. It adapted to environment changes and survived for almost a million years.

THE HANDY MAN

The fossilized remains of another early human that lived from 2.4 to 1.4 million years ago were discovered in 1960 in the Olduvai Gorge in Tanzania. Named *Homo habilis* ("handy man"), this species had a slightly larger skull (brain) and was capable of making stone tools.

In 2005, in Dmanisi in the Eastern European nation of Georgia, a well-preserved skull, 1.8 million years old, of an ancient prehuman was excavated and named "Skull 5."[4] The remains of four other individuals who lived at the same time were also found. Researchers think that these remains are connected to *Homo habilis*.

In 2013, evidence of another prehuman was found in Western Europe when a fossilized molar was uncovered at Barranco León in the Orce region of southeastern Spain.[5] It dates to about 1.4 million years ago.

WALKING ERECT

Homo erectus ("erect man") is considered a descendant of *Ardipithecus ramidus*, *Australopithecus afarensis*, and *Homo habilis*. By about five hundred thousand years ago, *Homo erectus* became well established in Africa, Europe, and Asia. It spread to different parts of the world, and its fossils have been found in Georgia, Spain, India, China, and Indonesia.

These short, stocky prehumans could stand and walk, learned to make fire about three hundred thousand years ago, and made tools. They became the ancestors of the Neanderthals who lived in Europe from about forty thousand to two hundred thousand years ago.

In 1891, a Dutch surgeon named Eugène Dubois found the *Homo erectus* fossil known as Java Man in Indonesia. During excavations near Peking (modern Beijing) between 1929 and 1937, researchers discovered several partial skulls of the species that lived around four hundred thousand years ago and came to be known as Peking Man. Another fossil of a humanlike species aged four hundred thousand years ago was discovered in the 1990's in Sima de

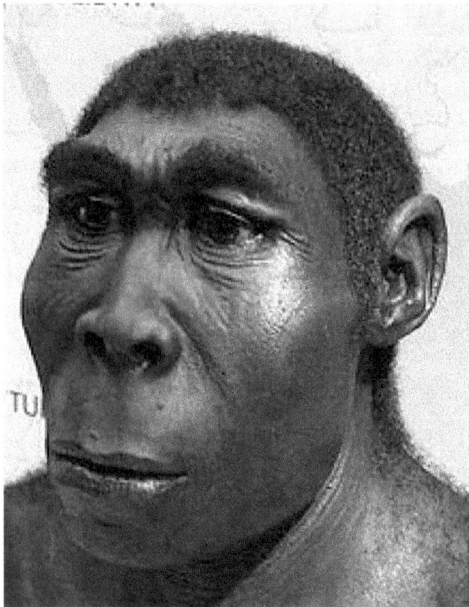

3.6 - Homo erectus

50

los Huesos ("pit of bones") in northern Spain.

In 1982, the partial fossilized skull of a hominid was recovered in Madhya Pradesh by Dr. Arun Sonakia of the Geological Survey of India.[6] The specimen was identified as a partial right-side cranium and

3.7 - Homo heidelbergenis

named *Homo erectus narmadensis* ("Narmada man"). It is approximately three hundred thousand years old and is the oldest hominid find from India. *Homo erectus* also lived on the Pothohar Plateau along the Soan River near modern-day Rawalpindi in Pakistan.[7]

Stone Age artifacts from one hundred to five hundred thousand years ago have been found in the Soan Valley in Pakistan. Hand axes found at Didwana in Rajasthan, similar to those from the Shivalik hills, date to about four hundred thousand years ago. These findings suggest a connection with the *Homo erectus* species on the Indian subcontinent during that period.

David G. Mahal

A fossil discovered in 1907 near Heidelberg in Germany was named *Homo heidelbergensis* by Otto Schoetensack. Since then, other fossils of this species have been found and dated from two hundred thousand to one million years ago. Researchers generally agree that *Homo heidelbergensis* evolved from *Homo erectus*. Similar fossils have been found in various parts of Africa, Europe, and Asia and are considered to be the direct ancestors of *Homo sapiens*—the modern human.

NEANDERTHALS AND DENISOVANS

Between three and four hundred thousand years ago, an ancestral group of prehumans left Africa and went in different directions. One branch ventured northwest into West Asia and Europe and became known as *Homo neanderthalensis* or Neanderthals. The other branch moved east and became known as *Denisova hominins* or Denisovans. According to one theory, Neanderthals, Denisovans, and modern humans are all descended from *Homo heidelbergensis*.

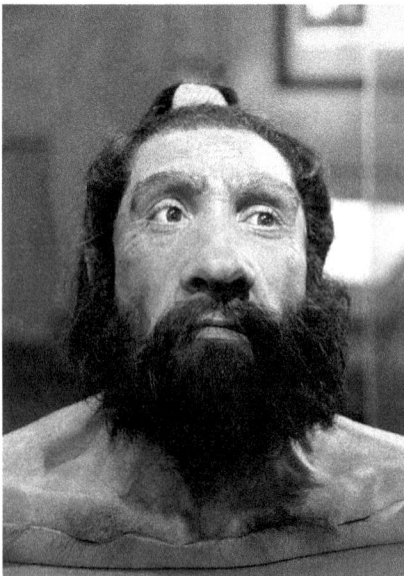

3.8 - Neanderthal

Although Neanderthals and Denisovans became extinct about thirty thousand years ago, genetic evidence shows that modern *Homo sapiens* interbred with them.[8]

HOMO SAPIENS

In 1967, a team led by Richard Leakey found two skulls and some bones on opposite sides of the Omo River in the Omo Kibish area of Ethiopia. The fossils, named Omo I and Omo II, were dated at about 190,000 years old.[9] The fossilized skulls of two other adults and one child were discovered near a village called Herto in the Afar region of Eastern Ethiopia and announced in 2003. Dated at 160,000 years old, these are the oldest known fossils of the recognizable modern humans (*Homo sapiens*) that were our direct ancestors.[10] Today, Ethiopia is considered the cradle of modern human civilization.

MIGRATIONS

It is a basic drive among living creatures to move around and seek better pastures for food and shelter. Birds, animals, and water dwellers have done it since time immemorial. Storks and cranes from the cold regions of Russia and China make the treacherous journey over the Himalayas to India during the winter months. Canadian geese fly long distances to winter in the southerly, warmer parts of North America. Even fragile, dainty monarch

3.9 Monarch butterflies

butterflies migrate by the millions to the warmer climates of California and Mexico every winter. Many types of whales swim toward the colder poles in the summer and toward the more tropical waters of the equator in the winter. Humans have done the same thing and populated the entire planet. It is happening to this day; legally or illegally, every year people migrate from less developed areas to more developed areas for better opportunities. It all started in Africa.

EMERGENCE OF MODERN HUMANS

There are two competing hypotheses in paleoanthropology (the study of human beginnings) regarding the origins of *Homo sapiens* or modern humans. One states that they migrated out of Africa about one hundred thousand years ago and that modern humans replaced older hominids (*Homo heidelbergensis*, *Homo neanderthalensis*, and Denisovans) in Europe and Asia by about fifty thousand years ago. The other hypothesis states that modern humans evolved in different parts of the world, but it allows for contributions from Africa.

According to Dr. Luigi Cavalli-Sforza, a noted Stanford University scholar, "From a geneticist's point of view, a single origin followed by expansion is the more credible of the two."[11] Research supports the "out of Africa" hypothesis. Scientists have compared 650,000 genetic markers in about a thousand individuals from fifty-one populations around the globe and concluded that modern humans gradually settled the world after leaving Africa.[12] Based on anatomical, archaeological, and genetic evidence, the current scientific explanation for the beginning of all modern humans is the model that claims an African origin.[13]

OUT OF AFRICA

We should note that the early humans were primitive people, just slightly ahead of the animals, searching for shelter in trees, caves, and huts. They walked into unknown territories and adapted to different climates. They lived on jungle produce or fish if they were close to water, and not all of them may have known how to make fire. They used sticks, stones, and bones to make tools and weapons. Research suggests that some groups practiced incest until they learned that it led to diseases and deformities. Some tribes, like those mentioned by Herodotus, engaged in cannibalism. They suffered natural calamities and encountered dangerous animals in their paths. Many perished due to diseases for which there were no cures.

The migrants out of Africa, between eighty and one hundred thousand years ago, eventually replaced the older hominid species. The initial migrants traveled north and crossed into the Arabian Peninsula. Some travelled further north into central Asia, which became the staging ground for migrations to Serbia and Europe.

Others traveled as beachcombers along the southern coast of the Arabian Peninsula. They moved east toward India and continued to Indonesia, Borneo, China, and Australasia. Along the way, humans interbred with Neanderthals and Denisovans. Genetic markers from these older human populations are found today in the gene pools of southern Chinese, New Guinean, and other Micronesian Island populations. These results suggest that modern humans underwent genetic changes involved with brain function, the nervous system, and language development.

Our planet was advancing into an ice age, which made the continents bigger and joined them in certain places. Walking a coastal route to the Far East and Australia was easier than it would be today. Some people continued northeast toward Siberia. There was an ice bridge between Siberia and Alaska at that time, and about twenty thousand years ago, people crossed this bridge and populated North and South America. Scientists believe that this initial group may have been as small as twenty people.

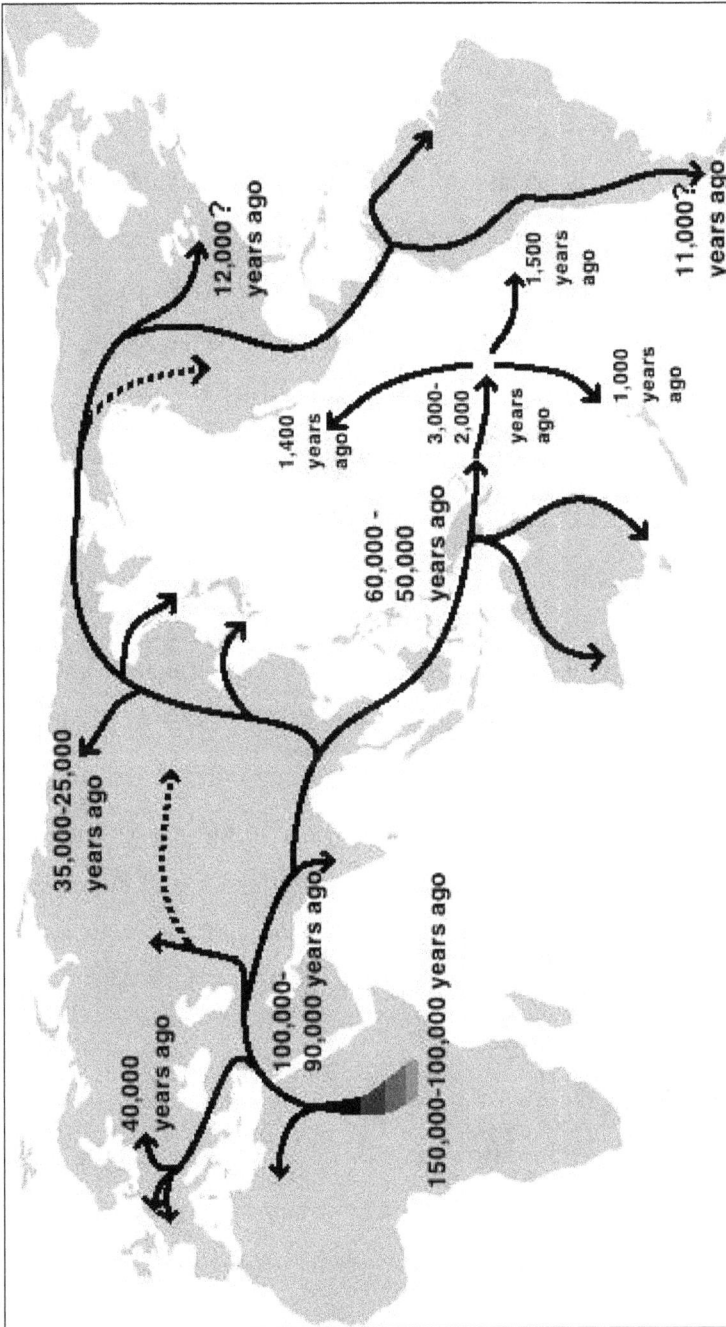

3.10 – Initial Migrations
(Map: National Institute for Genetics, Japan)

David G. Mahal

The migration through India was interrupted about seventy-four thousand years ago by the eruption of Mount Toba in Sumatra, Indonesia. This was one of the largest volcanic eruptions in this planet's history. The catastrophe caused a six-year nuclear winter and a thousand-year ice age. North Atlantic surface temperatures and global sea levels dropped significantly. Volcanic ash up to twenty feet deep covered the Indian subcontinent, and the population of the region fell dramatically. As the result, the human population on the planet may have dropped to about two thousand people and almost become extinct.[14]

Michael Petraglia and his team from the University of Cambridge discovered stone tools at a site called Jwalapuram in Andhra Pradesh, South India, above and below a thick layer of ash from the Toba eruption. This suggests that life continued for humans living in the area.[15] A warming of the climate allowed repopulation of the area. New migrations out of Africa from about fifty thousand years ago populated India with large numbers of humans who later became known as Dravidians.

Another reliable record of modern humans in the area was the recent discovery of the *Homo sapiens balangodensis* (Balangoda man) in Sri Lanka. The specimen is dated to about thirty-seven thousand years ago.[16] This finding is consistent with records of other anatomically modern humans in Asia from this period.

Since 2005, the National Geographic Society has conducted the Genographic Project to analyze and better understand historical patterns in human DNA from participants around the world. A study headed by Dr. Ramasamy Pitchappan of Chettinad University, who served as the regional director of Genographic India, found that people living in villages near Madurai in South India carried the same rare genetic markers as some Australian aborigines and people living in Africa. The finding showed a link between the three continents and confirmed that the people in Australia and India who carried this genetic marker were likely descendants of the original coastal migrants from Africa.[17]

It should be noted that the migrations out of Africa did not proceed in straight lines. After people settled an area, clans formed and then dispersed in different directions. The clans grew in size and clashed with each other for power and territorial rights. Some backtracked and returned to their original areas. Over thousands of years, populations increased everywhere. Improved tools and weapons were created, and wars broke out between people. Leaders emerged, and kingdoms and empires came into existence.

PHYSICAL CHANGES IN PEOPLE

Human skin color ranges from the darkest brown-black to the lightest white. If all human ancestors emigrated from Africa, how did they lose the dark-brown pigmentation in their skin?

Skin pigmentation changed because of the amount of ultraviolet radiation (UVR) penetrating the skin in different parts of the world. Areas at or near the equator with higher amounts of UVR have dark-skinned people, and areas closer to the north and south poles have lower concentrations of UVR and lighter-skinned people. People in northern Europe receive extremely low levels of UVR during their long, dark winters, whereas countries around the equator receive UVR throughout the year.

Light or dark skin is also related to the production of vitamin D from sunlight. People with lighter skin absorb vitamin D from sunlight more easily than those with dark skin. Dark skin prevents damage from the sun, and light skin lets in more sun and triggers production of vitamin D.

Research suggests that skin color changed from dark to light (and vice versa) as people migrated to different UVR zones during the last fifty thousand years.[18] The admixture between different populations resulted in the different skin pigmentations we see today. Height and other physical differences are attributed to differences in food and climate from one region to another.

THE SUMMARY, SO FAR

From what we know today, the universe is about 13.7 billion years old. The Earth and its solar system are about 4.55 billion years old, and life started from microscopic beginnings more than three billion years ago.

The oldest prehuman remains discovered so far are about six million years old. Modern humans evolved in Africa about two hundred thousand years ago and migrated to the rest of the world during the last one hundred thousand years.

Humans started speaking languages about one hundred thousand years ago. The first written languages were developed about five thousand years ago, and historians started documenting history only during the last 2500 years or so.

Since life began on Earth, there have been at least five mass extinctions when more than 50 percent of the animal species died. The last event, attributed to the impact of an asteroid, took place about sixty-six million years ago. The monstrous dinosaurs we saw in the Jurassic Park movies were a part of this extinction. The human population almost became extinct after the Mount Toba eruption nearly seventy four thousand years ago.

We don't know everything about our own species, but through studies of the universe, fossils, genetics, behavior, and biology, we continue to learn more about our past and who we are today.

CHAPTER 4

MIGRATIONS AND WARFARE

"People will not look forward to posterity who never look backward to their ancestors."— Edmund Burke

Although the migrations out of Africa to India and beyond initially proceeded along the coast, some migrants spread to the inner parts of the subcontinent. It is believed that the new migrants bred with the older *Homo erectus* species as evidenced by the Narmada Man that existed in India as long as three hundred thousand years ago. Later, there were waves of incursions into India over thousands of years and people came from different geographical areas.

Many migrations were peaceful, and many were extremely violent with massacres of large numbers of people who were already there. The arrivals multiplied and created a large population in India. A review of these migrations and invasions will help us develop insights into the foreign influences and diverse groups that populated India.

We should keep in mind that peaceful migrations usually include families and children, but invaders normally do not travel with their wives and children. Many of them may not even have families. After killing the men opposing them, the winning marauders tended to take the local women and rape and/or marry them. This has been the case during wars everywhere. Many invaders go back to where they came from, taking their loot with them, and others settle in the conquered area and create new families. In this manner, foreign and indigenous genes are mixed. The following pages deal only glancingly with Indian history; the focus is to illustrate the diversity of people who came to this land.

30,000 BCE: BHIMBETKA CAVES

In 1957–58, Indian archaeologist Dr. Vishnu Wakankar discovered prehistoric rock shelters in Bhimbetka near Bhopal in Madhya Pradesh. Named a World Heritage Site by the United Nations Educational, Scientific, and Cultural Organization (UNESCO) in 2003, Bhimbetka has more than seven hundred rock shelters with more than four hundred paintings carved in stone.

Some of these shelters were inhabited by the *Homo erectus* species more than three hundred thousand years ago.[1] Many other people lived in the shelters over the years. Although not fully corroborated, according to the Archaeological Survey of India, the name Bhimbetka is derived from Bhima (the second of the five

David G. Mahal

Pandava brothers named in the Mahabharata) who stayed in the caves at one time.[2]

The stone art is more than thirty thousand years old and among the oldest known rock art sites (the Chauvet Cave paintings in France go back thirty-seven thousand years, and the newly discovered El Castillo cave paintings in Spain are 40,800 years old).

4.1 - Bhimbetka Rock Art

The art was produced over a long period. The colors used are from vegetables. The art has endured over a long period of time because the drawings were made deep inside the caves. More recent artwork shows horses or similar animals and the riders holding what appear to be spears or weapons. The artwork suggests that domesticated horses and similar animals existed in the area in the distant past.

7000 BCE: INDUS VALLEY CIVILIZATION

Also known as the Harappan Civilization, the Indus Valley Civilization arose in northwestern India. Major sites of this period include Mehrgarh, Harappa, Mohenjo Daro, Dholavira, Ganeriwala, Rakhigarhi, Rupar, and Lothal. Some sites are now in Pakistan, and some are in India. Originally thought to

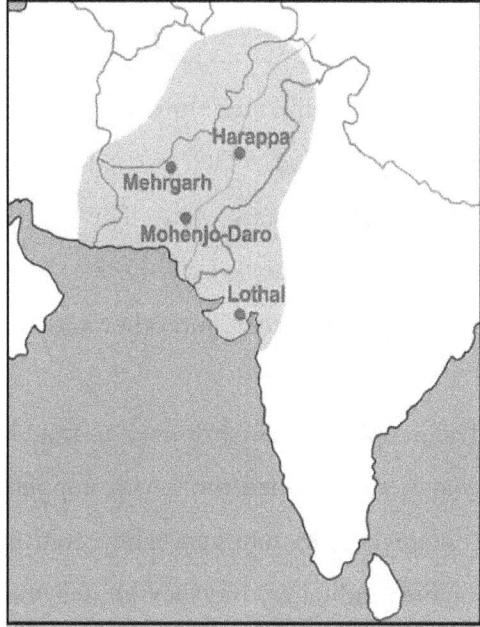

4.2 - Indus Civilization

have evolved around 3750 BCE, research has pushed the origin of this civilization back several thousand years. At the International Conference on Harappan Archaeology held by the Archaeological Survey of India in Chandigarh in 2012, it was announced that on the basis of radiometric dates and excavations at sites in Pakistan and India, "the cultural remains of the pre-Harappan horizon go back to 7380 BC to 6201 BC."[3]

Mehrgarh, another UNESCO World Heritage Site, lies in the Kachi plain of Balochistan in Pakistan. The site was discovered in

David G. Mahal

1974 by French archaeologists Jean-François and Catherine Jarrige, and it is older than the pyramids of Giza. Mounds discovered in the area show that humans buried their dead thousands of years ago. The Jarriges also unearthed clay pots, ornaments, buildings, and other items.

4.3 - Indus Pottery

The people of Mehrgarh lived in mud brick houses, stored grain in granaries, fashioned tools with copper ore, and lined large basket containers with bitumen. They cultivated barley, einkorn, wheat, jujubes, and dates, and they herded sheep, goats, and cattle. Horse bones have been found in the ruins. These were probably the earliest agriculturists in South Asia.[4]

4.4 - Indus Priest/King

The site was occupied continuously until about 2600 BCE.[5] Residents directed their efforts into crafts including tanning, bead production, and metalworking. There is evidence that the people had contact with cultures in northern Afghanistan, northeastern Iran, and southern central Asia and carried on commerce with Arabia.[6]

4.5 - Mehrgarh Houses

An advanced urban culture is evident in the Indus Valley Civilization. The quality of town layouts suggests the knowledge of urban planning and government that placed a high priority on hygiene. Water was obtained from wells, some homes had a room set aside for bathing, and wastewater was directed to covered drains.

The people of this civilization were among the first to develop a system of uniform weights and measures. In 2001, archaeologists studying the remains of two men from Mehrgarh discovered a tradition of protodentistry in the early farming cultures of that region.[7]

David G. Mahal

The origin of the Indus Valley people is not clear. Because of their contact with cultures in Afghanistan, Iran, Arabia, and south central Asia, they may have originated from one or more of these areas. Some scholars claim that they were indigenous Dravidians.

As the result of climate change and probably the arrival of Aryans from the north, these people eventually abandoned the Indus Valley and shifted to other parts of India.

There are no concrete records, but the world population in 5000 BCE is estimated to be about five million.[8] On this basis, the estimated population of the entire Indian subcontinent at that time, including the Indus Valley, was only about one million (assuming it was 20 percent of the total).

4.6 – Mohenjo Daro

6000 BCE: KETAVARAM CAVES

A group of cave paintings has been discovered in Ketavaram in the Kurnool district of Andhra Pradesh in South India. According to the Archaeology Department of Pondicherry, these paintings are more than six thousand years old, and some are contemporary to the Indus Valley Civilization.

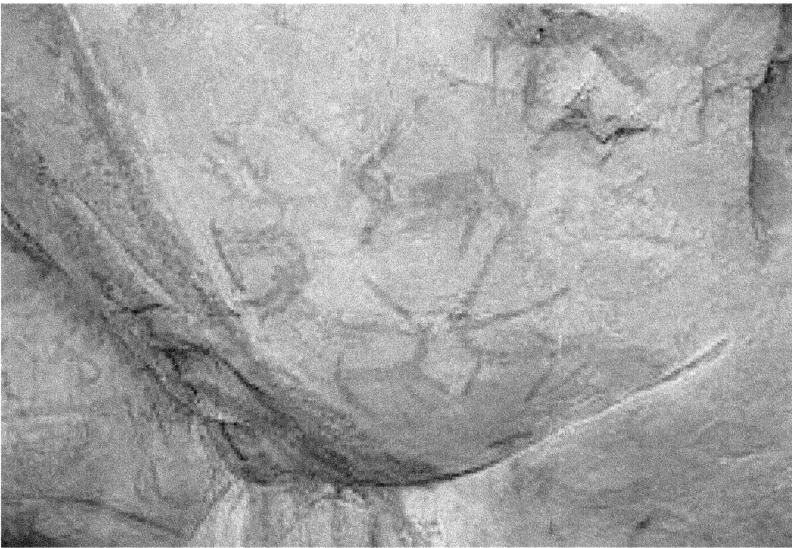

4.7 - Ketavaram Rock Art

5000 BCE: EDAKKAL CAVES

The Edakkal Caves are located in the Wayanad district of Kerala in the Western Ghats of South India. There are pictorial writings, human and animal figures, symbols, and drawings of various types, all of which are dated to 5000 BCE. Some historians believe that the people of this area were originally from the Indus Valley Civilization and moved to South India.[9, 10]

4.8 - Edakkal Rock Art

4000 BCE: INDO-ARYANS

Located between the Caspian and the Aral Seas, the Amu Darya or Oxus River runs from the Pamir Mountains and generally forms the border between Tajikistan, Afghanistan, Uzbekistan, and Turkmenistan. The Bactria–Margiana Archaeological Complex (BMAC) located in a site called Gonur represents a Bronze Age civilization, known as the Oxus Civilization, of around 4000 BCE. These sites were discovered and named by the Soviet archaeologist Viktor Sarianidi. Driven by what appears to be ecological changes, the people of this civilization moved southwest to Iran and southeast to India through the Hindu Kush mountain range. They were called Aryans ("noble" or "civilized" ones in Sanskrit), and those who came into India became known as Indo-Aryans.

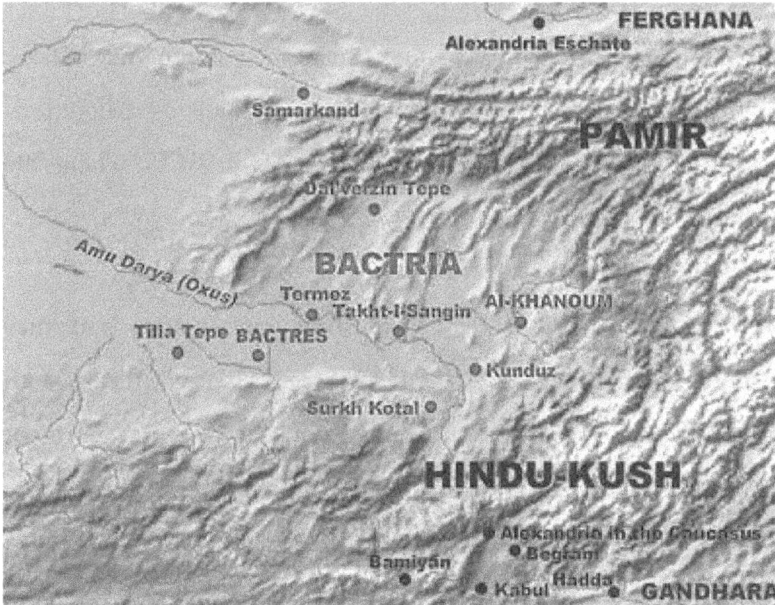
4.9 - Bactria-Margiana

Although there are different opinions about the origin of these people, the BMAC is considered a major settlement for their ancestors. Among his findings, Sarianidi discovered evidence of sacred altars; traces of ingredients such as poppy seeds, cannabis, and ephedra, used for a drink called *soma*; horse sacrifices; four-wheeled chariots; and other connections with the Aryan teachings.[11]

BMAC materials have been found in the Indus Valley sites as well. Academics like Asko Parpola, an Indologist at the University of

71

David G. Mahal

Helsinki in Finland, and J. P. Mallory, an archaeologist from Queens University in Ireland and editor of the *Journal of Indo-European Studies*, have also associated the Aryans to the BMAC.[12]

Aryans came to India in waves and brought with them what are known as Indo-Aryan or Indo-European languages. Migrations into the Indus Valley started around 1500 BCE when the civilization began to decline.

The nomadic Aryans were a cattle-breeding society, and they settled in northwest India as agriculturists. They conflicted with the indigenous people and pushed them out to other parts of India. Somewhere along the line, the Aryans domesticated the elephant, which was used in battles with Alexander the Great.

Aryans integrated the Indus culture into their own to form what came to be known as the Vedic culture. This civilization is associated with four texts known as the Vedas ("knowledge" or "wisdom"), and these became the sacred texts of Hinduism, the third-largest religion in the world. The first text, the *Rig Veda*, contains 1,028 verses; the other three are the *Sama Veda*, the *Yajur Veda*, and the *Atharva Veda*. The Vedas contain hymns (verses in praise of gods), philosophy, and other guidance. They represent the oldest teachings of India, though the transmission of these teachings was mainly oral until around CE 500 when they were written in Sanskrit.

The caste system in India refers to a stratified social hierarchy. It is generally attributed to the Aryans. The *Rig Veda* mentions four castes: Brahman, Rajanya, Vaisya, and Sudra. Based on an individual's profession and duties, this type of social division became the Hindu *varna* system. The Brahman were the priests and teachers, the Rajanya (later known as the Kshatriya) were the ruling class and warriors, the Vaisya represented the merchants and agriculturists, and the Sudra were the general working class including servants. Certain groups, later known as Dalits or the "untouchables," were excluded from the *varna* system.

There is controversy about the origin of the Aryans. Some Indian academics claim that speakers of the Indo-Aryan languages are

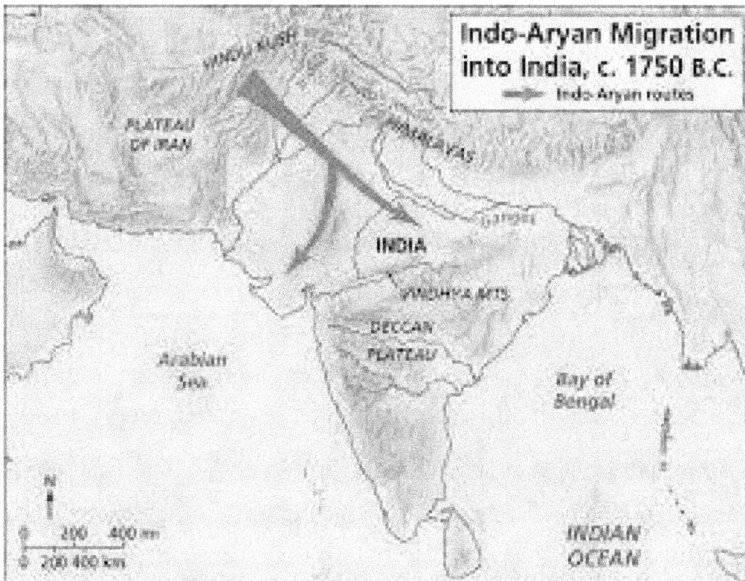

4.10 - Aryan Migration

indigenous to the Indian subcontinent and that Indo-European languages originated in India. A recent study by Indian geneticists from the Centre for Cellular and Molecular Biology (CCMB) in Hyderabad reported that the widely believed theory of Aryan invasions is a myth. "Our study clearly shows that there was no genetic influx 3,500 years ago," according to Dr. Kumarasamy Thangaraj of CCMB. He led the research team that included scientists from the University of Tartu, Chettinad Academy of Research and Education in Chennai, and Banaras Hindu University (BHU). "It is high time we re-write India's prehistory based on scientific evidence," said Dr. Lalji Singh, former director of CCMB, former vice chancellor of BHU, and coauthor of the study. "There is no genetic evidence that Indo-Aryans invaded or migrated to India or even something such as Aryans existed." [13]

As we will see in a later section, the genes of many people in India can be traced back to the BMAC area and central Asia.

550 BCE: PERSIAN INFLUENCE

The First Persian Empire, also known as the Achaemenid Empire, was founded by Cyrus the Great (559–530 BCE). This empire stretched from Thrace and Macedon on the northeastern border of Greece to the Indus Valley. After Cyrus, the kingdom was ruled by Darius I (521–486 BCE). The Persians ruled Taxila, now in Pakistan, during this period.

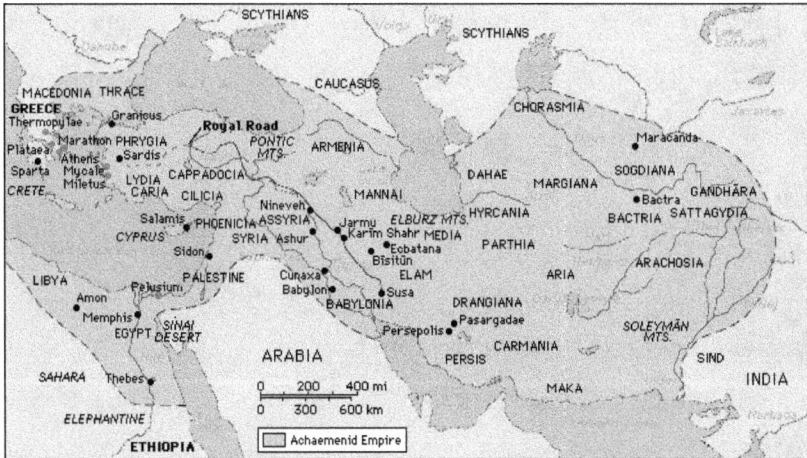

4.11 - The Persian Empire

326 BCE: ALEXANDER THE GREAT

At the age of thirty, Alexander the Great (356–323 BCE) began his invasion into India in 326 BCE. One year later, he fought an epic battle against the Indian king Porus of the Hindu Paurava kingdom on the banks of the Jhelum River in Punjab, now in Pakistan. After his victory, he made an alliance with Porus and appointed him a Macedonian satrap (local ruler).

Alexander appointed some Greek forces in Taxila and conquered areas around the Indus River down to the Arabian Sea. He sent a large contingent of his army to Carmania (modern southern Iran) with his general, Craterus, and he commissioned a fleet to explore the Persian Gulf shore under his admiral, Nearchus.

David G. Mahal

Alexander was critically injured during his attack on Multan, now in Pakistan. After a brief period of convalescence, he led his forces back to Persia by the southern route through the Gedrosia (modern Makran in southern Pakistan).

After his death in 323 BCE, a series of fierce struggles among his followers destroyed his empire, and the territories were divided among his generals. One of the commanders, Seleucus, established himself in Babylon. He expanded his territory as far as the western portions of India under what became known as the Seleucid Empire.

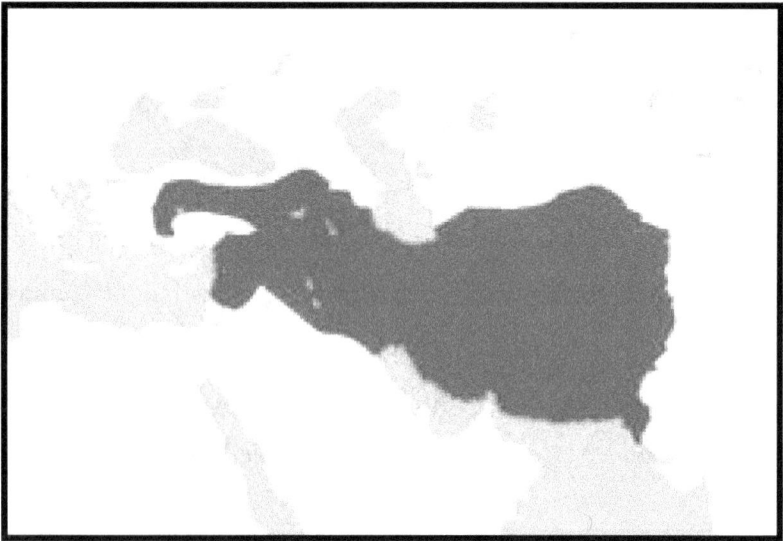

4.12 - After Alexander, Seleucid Empire

326 BCE: ARMENIANS

Armenians are believed to have arrived in India after Alexander's army crossed Armenia en route to India. It appears that more arrived later. They formed communities and flourished as merchants and traders in several parts of India. A small community still remains in Kolkata.[14]

4.13 - Armenian Holy Church, Kolkota

322–185 BCE: MAURYAN EMPIRE

Chandragupta Maurya (r. 322–298 BCE), a contemporary of Alexander the Great and one of the greatest leaders in Indian history, was the first emperor to unify India into one state. He became well known for conquering Alexander's eastern satrapies (areas controlled by a local ruler) and for defeating Seleucus in battle. Chandragupta and Seleucus reached an agreement about the border, formalized an alliance, and established a policy of friendship. Chandragupta ended up marrying Seleucus's daughter,

Helen, bringing Greek genes into his offspring. Thus, Chandragupta's son, Bindusara (r. 298–272 BCE), and grandson, Ashoka (r. 268-232 BCE), another great emperor in the history of India, were partly Greek.

Seleucus sent Megasthenes, a historian and diplomat, as his ambassador to the court of Chandragupta. Megasthenes wrote a detailed account of India, the *Indica*, in four volumes, most of which are lost. Among many things, he mentioned there were seven castes in Indian society during this time (compared to four in the *Rig Veda* during the Aryan period).

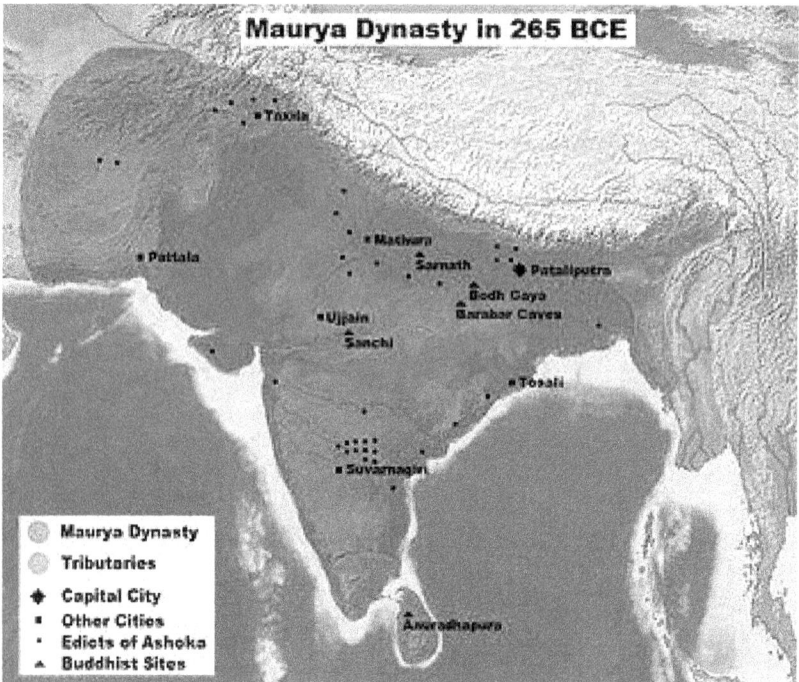

4.14 - The Mauryan Empire

4.15 - Ashoka's Lion Pillar

Under Chandragupta's rule, almost all parts of India became united under a single government, thus establishing the Mauryan Empire. At that time, Indian borders touched Persia and central Asia. He conquered Gandhara and made several areas of the northwest parts of India. After many conquests, Chandragupta resigned, became a Jain monk, and ended his life by ritually fasting to death.

His son, Bindusara, assumed the throne and ruled India for many years. Bindusara's son, Ashoka, conquered more territories. After seeing the enormous death and destruction he caused in the Kalinga War, he stopped the policy of conquering new areas. He became a Buddhist and started to follow the path of *ahimsa* (not to injure). He sent persons to several parts of India, China, and Sri Lanka to preach Buddhism. Ashoka ruled most of India as it stands today. He built a number of stupas and pillars with inscriptions of his understanding of Buddhist doctrines. His lion

David G. Mahal

pillar is the emblem of India today. Brihadratha (r. 187–185 BCE) was the last ruler of the Mauryan Empire.

Kautalya, also known as Chanakya (Chanakyapuri, the diplomatic enclave of New Delhi, is named after him), guided Chandragupta Maurya and his sons in founding and expanding the great Mauryan Empire. He composed the *Arthashastra*, a treatise on statecraft, economic policy, and military strategy (it includes the memorable saying, "My enemy's enemy is my friend"). This work was written in Taxila, several hundred years before Niccolò Machiavelli composed a similar treatise, *The Prince,* in Italy.

200–100 BCE: JEWS ARRIVE IN INDIA

By this time, trade routes from the Mediterranean to South India were well established. A group of Jewish traders arrived and settled in Cochin, Kerala.

Another group arrived at about the same time and settled in the Mumbai

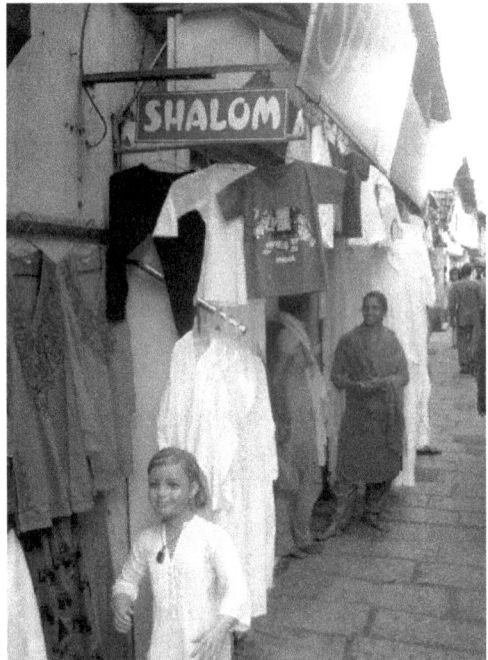

4.16 Jew Town, Cochin
(Copyright © David G. Mahal)

area. Although many Indian Jews have immigrated to Israel in recent years, small communities still thrive in Cochin and some other cities of India.

200 BCE TO CE 10: GREEKS IN NORTH INDIA

After the Mauryan dynasty, Indo-Greeks, who were remnants of Alexander the Great's forces, returned to power in various parts of northwestern India. They ruled from about 200 BCE to CE 10 and were eventually conquered by the Indo-Scythians and Kushans. A part of the following timeline is based on an extensive study of excavated coins from this period by Sri Lankan historian and numismatist Osmund Bopearachchi.[15]

Demetrius I (r. 200–190 BCE) was the first ruler and founder of the Indo-Greek kingdom.

Menander I (r. 155–130 BCE) ruled over the eastern divided Greek empire of Bactria along with the northwest Frontier Province and Punjab in Pakistan, Punjab, Haryana, and parts of Himachal Pradesh and the Jammu region in present-day India. His capital is supposed to have been modern Sialkot in Pakistan.

Based on one of his coins, Thraso (possibly ruled around 130 BCE) was an Indo-Greek king in central and western Punjab. Philoxenus Anicetus (r. 125–110 BCE) was an Indo-Greek king who ruled in the region spanning the Paropamisadae (the ancient Greek name for a region of the Hindu-Kush in eastern Afghanistan) to Punjab.

Agathokleia Theotropos (r. 110–100 BCE) was an Indo-Greek queen who ruled in parts of northern India as regent for her son,

4.17 - Menander Silver Coin

Strato I. Although not fully corroborated, after losing some territory, Strato I (r. 110–85 BCE) is believed to have ruled over Gandhara and western Punjab.

Artemidoros Aniketos (possibly ruled around 100–80 BCE) was a king who ruled the areas of Gandhara and Pushkalavati in modern northern Pakistan and Afghanistan.

Epander (r. 95–90 BCE) was an Indo-Greek king whose coins seem to indicate that he ruled the area of Punjab. Heliocles II (r. 95–80 BCE) was another Indo-Greek king who ruled over parts of the northwest. Archebios (r. 90–70 BCE) ruled the area of Taxila. Telephos Euergetes (r. 75–70 BCE) was a late Indo-Greek king in Gandhara who appears to have been a brief successor of Maues.

Strato II and III (r. 25 BCE to CE 10) ruled in eastern Punjab and retained Sialkot as the capital.

120 BCE: Yuezhi Incursions

The first significant appearance of the Xiongnu, fierce nomadic people who were likely the ancestors of the Huns, was in central China around 300 BCE. The Great Wall of China, which is about thirteen thousand miles long, was built in part to protect the Chinese Empire against intrusions from such nomadic groups. The Chinese were successful and repelled an invasion of the Xiongnu, pushing them toward the west.

4.18 The Great Wall of China
(Copyright: © David G. Mahal)

David G. Mahal

The Xiongnu turned their attention toward the Yuezhi, an ancient people who originally settled in what is today Xinjiang and western Gansu in China. The Yuezhi were driven west by the Xiongnu to the borderlands of what is now Afghanistan, Pakistan, Tajikistan, and Uzbekistan, where they established an independent empire in the region known as Bactria. In Bactria, they conquered the Scythians and the local Indo-Greek kingdoms, the last of Alexander the Great's forces that had failed to take India.

Early in the second century, the Yuezhi began to appear in the Oxus Valley (modern Amu Darya). They defeated the Scythians who occupied the area and pushed them south. Of the five Yuezhi chieftains, one branch founded the Kushan Empire, which

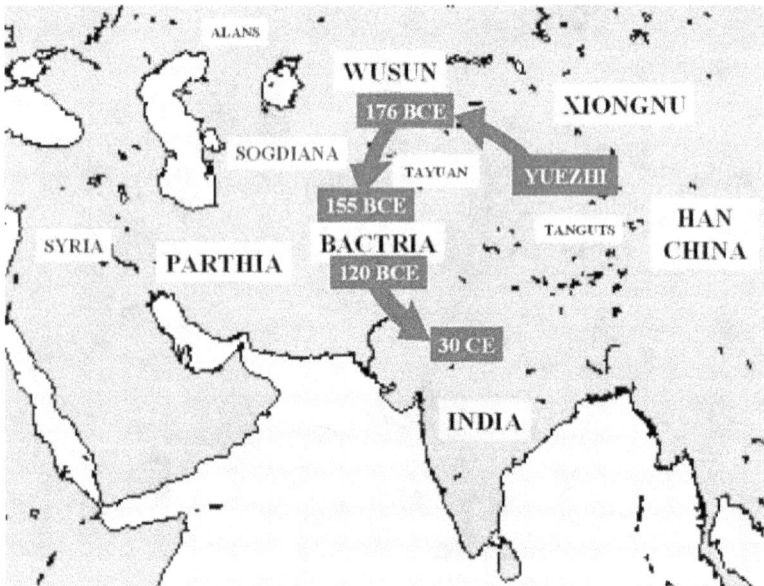

4.19 - Yuezhi Migrations

extended its power south and east into India and north into central Asia.

110 BCE TO CE 395: INDO-SCYTHIANS

Scythians (also called Sakas) were nomadic people who migrated from central Asia to southern Russia in the eighth and seventh centuries BCE. They developed a class of wealthy aristocrats, known as Royal Scyths, who ruled southern Russian and Crimean territories. The Persian king Darius I attacked these territories in about 513 BCE and was unsuccessful. The community was destroyed in the second century BCE, and it dispersed in different directions.

The term "Indo-Scythian" is used to refer to Scythians who migrated into parts of central Asia and south Asia from the middle of the second century BCE. The initial migration of the Scythians led them to Kashmir. More Scythians came to India from Siberia, passing through Bactria, Sogdiana, Kashmir, and Afghanistan.

After entering the Indian subcontinent through Afghanistan, the first Indo-Scythian kingdom occupied the southern areas from Sindh in Pakistan to Gujarat in India from around 110–80 BCE. These people gradually moved north into **Indo-Greek** territory, defeated the Indo-Greek rulers of northwest India, and established an Indo-Scythian kingdom in India.[16]

Based in Gandhara, the first Indo-Scythian king was Maues (r. 85–
60 BCE). Also known as Moga, he ruled over most of
northwestern India. After the death of Azes, the last king, Indo-
Scythian rule declined during the latter part of the first century
BCE. A number of minor leaders continued in local strongholds.
The Indo-Scythian kingdom ended in CE 395 when Chandragupta
II killed the last ruler.

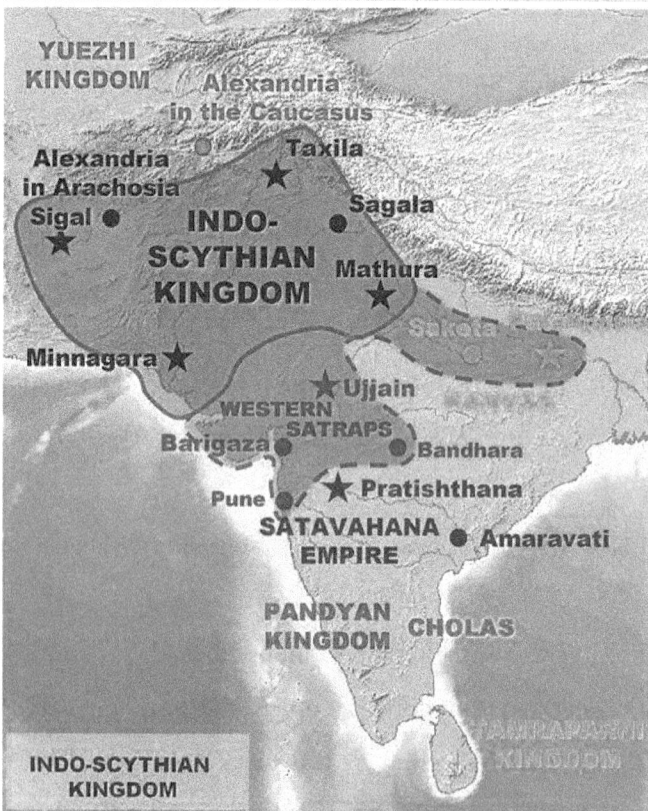

4.20 - Indo-Scythian Rule

80 BCE TO CE 200: INDIAN SPICE TRADE WITH EUROPE

4.21 - Spices

In 80 BCE, the markets of the Egyptian city of Alexandria were full of Indian spices en route to markets in Greece and the Roman Empire. In 21 BCE, a Tamil embassy was sent from Madurai to Rome. Indian spice trade with Rome reached its height in CE 100–200. The Archaeology Department of India has found one hundred thousand Roman coins in the Cauvery River delta, in southern India, along the old spice trade route.[17]

CE 30–335: THE KUSHAN EMPIRE

The Kushan Empire was formed in the early first century CE under Kujula Kadphises in the territories around the Oxus River (Amu Darya) and later near Kabul, Afghanistan. The Kushans spread from the Kabul River valley to defeat central Asian tribes that had conquered parts of the north central Iranian Plateau, once ruled by the Parthians. They reached their peak under the Buddhist emperor Kanishka (Yuezhi ethnicity), whose realm stretched from Turfan in the Tarim Basin to Pataliputra (modern Patna) in India.

David G. Mahal

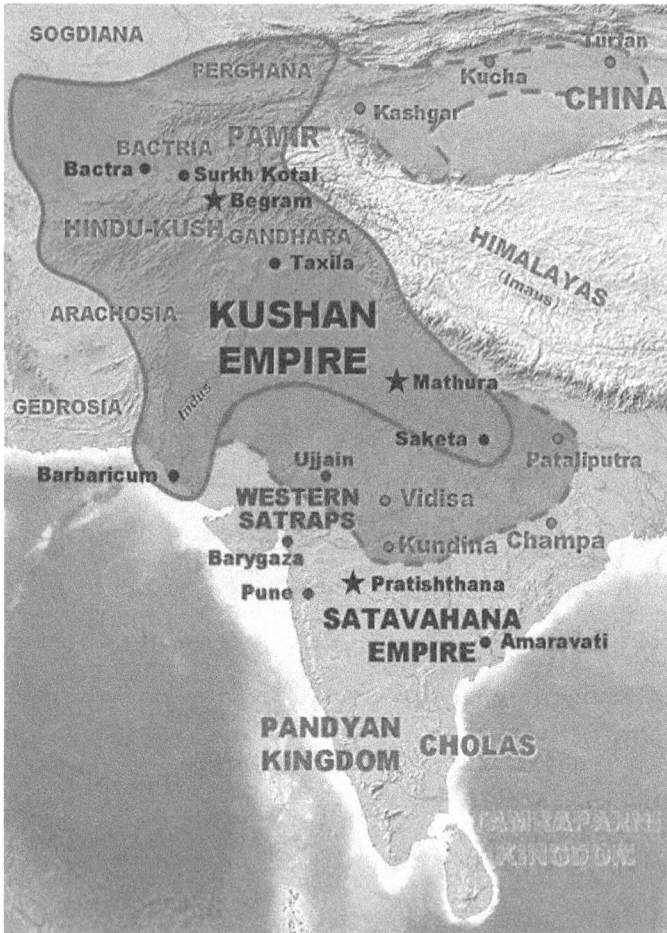

4.22 - Kushan Empire

Predominantly Zoroastrian, the Kushans incorporated Buddhist and Hellenistic beliefs into their religious practices. Kushan coins depict deities ranging from Helios and Heracles to the Buddha, Ahura Mazda, Mithra, and Atar, the Zoroastrian fire god. They used the Greek alphabet and altered it to suit spoken Kushan. The last of the Kushans were overwhelmed by the White Huns.

CE 52: ARRIVAL OF CHRISTIANITY

Saint Thomas, one of the twelve apostles of Jesus Christ, arrived in Muziris on the Kerala coast around CE 52 to convert the Jews of Kerala. Regarded as the patron saint of India, he is said to have founded the first Christian church in Kerala and six other places on the Malabar Coast. He was killed in CE 72 and buried at Saint Thomas Basilica in Chennai.[18]

CE 127–151: KANISHKA THE GREAT

Under Kanishka, the Kushan Empire expanded into northern India. Kanishka ruled from Peshawar, now in Pakistan, and the major Silk Road (trade routes in Asia) cities of Kashgar, Yarkand, and Khotan in what is now Xinjiang or east Turkestan. Kanishka was a devout Buddhist and has been compared to the Mauryan emperor Ashoka the Great. Evidence suggests that he worshipped the Persian deity Mithra, who was both a judge and a god of plenty.

After CE 225, the Kushan Empire crumbled into a western half that was almost immediately conquered by the Sassanid Empire of Persia and an eastern half with its capital in the Punjab. The eastern Kushan Empire fell, likely between CE 335 and 350, to the Gupta king Samudragupta.

David G. Mahal

CE 337–422: FA-HIEN

The Chinese Buddhist monk Fa-Hien traveled by foot from China to India to acquire Buddhist scriptures. During his travels, he visited Buddhist sites in China, Pakistan, India, Nepal, Bangladesh, and Sri Lanka, where a cave is named after him. He was in India during the reign of Chandragupta II.

CE 500: INVASION OF THE HUNS

The Huns were descendants of the Xiongnu, a group of fierce, warlike, nomadic herdsmen from the steppes of north central Asia, north of China (Mongolia). They pushed the Yuezhi out of the area, and during their migrations, they split into two groups.

One group went as far as Scythia, modern-day southern Russia and Kazakhstan, where they conquered a number of local tribes. Attila the Hun (CE 406–453) and his warriors rose from the plains of Scythia and spread terror across Europe. The European Huns settled in what is now Hungary.

Another group, later called the White Huns (in Greek, Hephthalites; in Sanskrit, Sveta Huna), moved into Afghanistan and made Bamiyan their capital city. Different from the Huns under Attila, the White Huns were believed to have white skin and elongated heads.

During the fifth century, the Gupta dynasty reigned in the Ganges basin of India, while the Kushan Empire occupied the area along the Indus. The Huns eventually conquered the Kushans. After the last of the Gupta rulers, Skandagupta, died in CE 467, they entered India and destroyed many cities and towns along the Ganges. They persecuted Buddhists and burned their monasteries. Their conquest was accomplished with extreme ferocity, and the Gupta regime was destroyed.

Based on their coins and inscriptions, Toramana and his son Mihirakula (Mehrgul) were the most famous Hun kings who ruled in northern India. Some historians believe that the Huns intermarried with the indigenous people and were absorbed in the Indian population.[19]

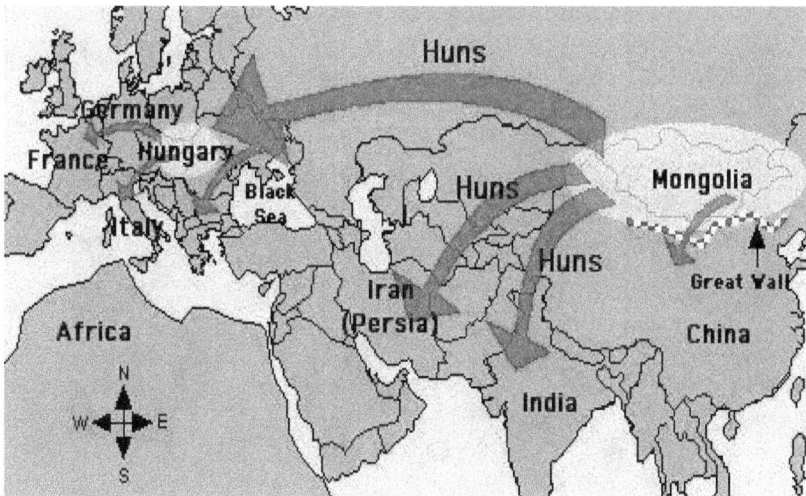

4.23 - Invasion of the Huns

David G. Mahal

CE 600–700: Arrival of Islam in South India

The Arabs were active mariners and traders throughout the Indian Ocean before the advent of Islam, and they had close ties with rulers of port cities along the Malabar Coast in South India. The Arabs introduced Islam to the people they traded with and constructed what is probably the first mosque in India in 628 in Kodungallur, Kerala. The mosque was built under the courtesy of the local king, Cheraman Perumal, who made a pilgrimage to Mecca and died during his return voyage.

The introduction of Islam to southern India was peaceful, contrary to the violent Islamic invasions and conversions that occurred later in northern India.

4.24 - Chermun Jama Masjid, Kerala

CE 627–643: Hiuen-Tsang

Another Chinese Buddhist monk, Hiuen-Tsang, made a difficult overland journey to India to acquire more sacred scriptures and books about Buddhism. He spent seventeen years in India, studied Buddhism at Nalanda University, and wrote a detailed account of his visit. The Hiuen-Tsang Memorial erected in his honor is one of the major tourist attractions in Nalanda.

CE 936: Arrival of the Parsees (Zoroastrians)

The origin of the Parsees ("Persians") can be traced to the Zoroastrian religion which was common throughout the Persian Empire by 500 BCE. From around CE 700 onward, Islam became the main religion of the area that is now Iran. A number of Zoroastrians left the area to escape persecution by the Muslim rulers and arrived in India in CE 936. Later, another wave migrated from Iran to India. The community thrives in the Mumbai area.

CE 971–1030: Mahmud of Ghazni

Of Turkish origin, Mahmud was born in Ghazni, Afghanistan, and he was the first ruler to carry the title of sultan ("authority"), signifying his power. He created an extensive empire which covered most of Afghanistan, eastern Iran, and northwest India. He invaded India seventeen times, plundered Hindu temples including the famous Somnath Temple in Gujarat, and killed thousands of people.

The court of Mahmud of Ghazni was a center of literature and poetry. Al-Biruni, a Persian scholar who distinguished himself in science and literature, played an important part as counselor to the sultan. He accompanied the sultan on his invasions and is said to have lived in India for thirteen years. He was the first Muslim scholar to study India, and he wrote *Tarikh Al-Hind* (History of India), also known as *Indica*, in which he detailed aspects of Indian culture. A crater on the moon is named after him.

1162–1227: GENGHIS KHAN

4.25 - Genghis Khan

In the early sixteenth century, descendants of Genghis Khan swept across the Khyber Pass and established the Mughal dynasty, which lasted for two hundred years.

Genghis Khan, the fearsome Mongolian warrior of the thirteenth century, may have done more than rule the largest empire in the world. According to a recently published genetic study, he may have helped increase the population as well. An international group of geneticists found that nearly 8 percent of the men living in the region of the former Mongol Empire carry genes that are nearly identical. That translates to 0.5 percent of the male population in the world or roughly sixteen million descendants living today.[20]

1206–1526: DELHI SULTANATE

The Delhi Sultanate refers to five short-lived Muslim dynasties of

Turkic and Afghan origin that ruled from Delhi. It was able to conquer most of northern and central India.

The first sultan of Delhi was Qutub-ud-din Aibak (1150–1210) of Turkic descent. In 1193, he commenced the construction of the Qutab Minar in

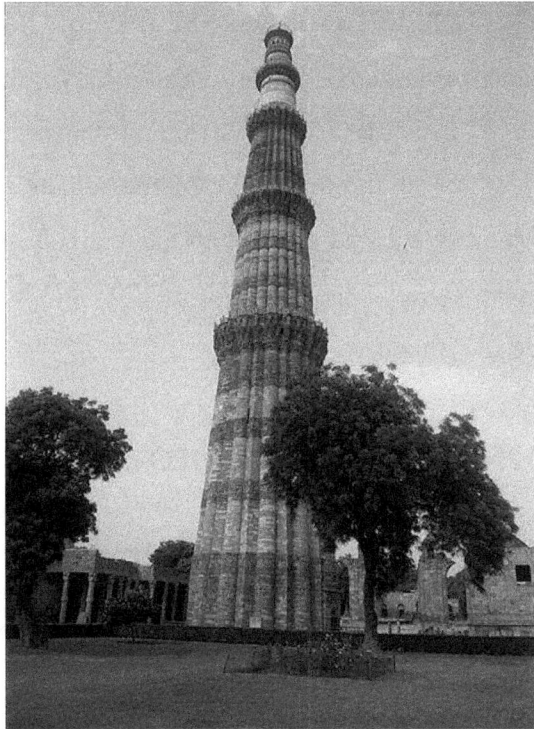

4.26 - Qutab Minar

Delhi, which became the first architectural work of Muslims in India. He ruled for four years (1206–1210) and died while playing polo.

He was followed by the Khilji, Tughlaq, and Sayyid dynasties. The last sultan of the Lodi dynasty was Ibrahim Lodi (r. 1517–1526), who ruled for nine years. He was killed in battle; this gave way to the Mughal Empire.

1236–1240: RAZIA SULTANA

The Delhi Sultanate was the only Indo-Muslim empire with a female ruler, Razia Sultana, who ruled for four years from 1236 to 1240. She was South Asia's first female Muslim ruler and the daughter of Iltutmish, one of the sultans of the Delhi Sultanate. She was talented, wise, brave, an excellent administrator, and a great warrior. She was born in 1205 and belonged to the Turkish Seljuks ancestry.

1254–1324: MARCO POLO

Marco Polo was a merchant traveler from Venice who sailed to China. He reported seeing fearsome tribes with heads of dogs in the Andaman Islands in the Bay of Bengal. It is not clear if he actually visited these islands or read about such tribes in the *Indika* of Ktesias (described in chapter 1).

Returning home in 1292, he arrived on the Coromandel Coast of India in a merchant ship with more than sixty cabins and up to three hundred crewmen. He entered the kingdom of the Tamil Pandyas near modern-day Thanjavur (formerly Tanjore). He documented this episode in his famous book, *The Travels*, with a rich description of India. His pioneering journeys inspired Christopher Columbus and other travelers.

1300: BAKHTIYAR KHILJI DYNASTY

In 1193, Nalanda was ransacked and destroyed by an army under the fanatic Bakhtiyar Khilji, a Turk. Khilji tried to uproot Buddhism and plant Islam by the sword. In the process, his army massacred thousands of Buddhist monks. The great library of Nalanda University is reported to have burned for three months after the invaders set fire to it. The Chinese monk Hiuen-Tsang, who studied at Nalanda, described a tall library building "soaring into the clouds." Following the destruction of the university, Buddhism lost its status as a major religion in India.

Attempts are underway to revive this ancient university; they are led by Amartya Sen, the Harvard economist and Nobel laureate, and academics from universities in Britain, China, Singapore, the United States, and Thailand. Offering programs in historical studies, ecology and environmental studies, Nalanda is one of the oldest centers of higher learning worldwide.

David G. Mahal

4.27 - Nalanda University Ruins

1336–1405: EMIR TIMUR

Timur, also known as Tamerlane ("Timur the Lame" in Turkish), was a Turkic ruler who conquered West, South, and central Asia and founded the Timurid dynasty. He emerged as a powerful Muslim ruler and referred to himself as the "Sword of Islam."

In 1398, he invaded North India and captured the Delhi Sultanate, which was under the Tughlaq dynasty at that time. His campaigns in India represented a systematic and barbaric slaughter of the local Hindu population. He justified his actions as a religious war and reportedly executed one hundred thousand captives. After plundering Delhi, he retired to Samarkand in Uzbekistan with many treasures and slaves from India.

1347–1527: BAHMANI SULTANATE

The Bahmani Sultanate was the first Muslim state of the Deccan in South India. It was founded by Allauddin Hassan, a Tajik, who broke away from the Delhi Sultanate. He ruled under the title Bahman Shah. There were eighteen rulers during the nearly two hundred years of this sultanate. They fought three battles with the Hindu Vijayanagara Empire to the south. They invited architects from Persia, Turkey, and Arabia to blend styles in constructing various buildings for the sultanate. The Charminar ("The Four Minarets"), a monument and mosque in Hyderabad, is one of several architectural tributes to the Bahmanis.

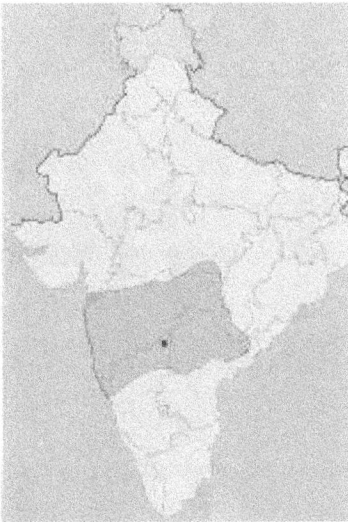

4.28 - Bahmani Sultanate

4.29 - Charminar

1494: SPANISH RIGHTS

To distribute trading and colonizing rights for all newly discovered lands between Portugal and Spain, in 1494, Pope Alexander VI gave Spain the territorial rights to India. These rights were removed less than a year later, and the Spanish did not follow through. However, the Portuguese felt differently.

1498: ARRIVAL OF THE PORTUGUESE

The Portuguese navigator Vasco da Gama pioneered the route from Europe to the Indian Ocean via the Cape of Good Hope in 1498 and paved the way for direct Indo-European commerce. The Portuguese arrived at Calicut in three ships and established the first European trading center at Kollam, Kerala.

Dom Afonso de Albuquerque was appointed the viceroy of India by King Emmanuel in 1509. The following year, he destroyed the Indian city of Calicut and took over Goa, claiming it for Portugal. He inaugurated the policy of marrying Portuguese soldiers and sailors to local Indian girls.

Another feature of the Portuguese presence was the will to promote Catholicism. The Portuguese soon set up trading posts in Goa, Daman, Diu, and Mumbai.

1527–1686: DECCAN SULTANATE

The Deccan Sultanate consisted of the kingdoms of Ahmednagar, Berar, Bidar, Bijapur, and Golkonda, located on the Deccan Plateau between the Krishna River and the Vindhya Range in southwestern India. These kingdoms became independent during the breakup of the Bahmani Sultanate and were eventually conquered by the Mughal Empire.

1527–1857: MUGHAL EMPIRE

The Mughal emperors were central Asian Turks from Uzbekistan who claimed to be descended from both Timur and Genghis Khan. Timur's great-great-grandson, Babur, founded the Islamic Empire and ruled over most of Afghanistan and North India. Babur's descendants (Humayun, Akbar, Jahangir, Shah Jahan, and Aurangzeb) expanded the Mughal Empire to most of the Indian subcontinent.

The greatest part of the Mughal expansion was accomplished during the reign of Akbar the Great (1556–1605), a freethinking Muslim, under whose rule the empire tripled in size and wealth. Akbar abolished the sectarian tax on non-Muslims, employed locals in his administration, and, to bring about religious unity, tried to create a new religion based on Islam, Hinduism,

David G. Mahal

Zoroastrianism, and Christianity. Padmini, a Hindu Rajput princess, became one of his many wives.

Sher Shah Suri (1486–1545), a Pashtun Afghan known as "The Lion King" (for reportedly killing a lion with his bare hands), rebelled against the Mughal rule and overthrew Babur's son, Humayun, in 1540. His short-lived sultanate in Delhi fell to Humayun again in 1555, and the Mughal Empire continued.

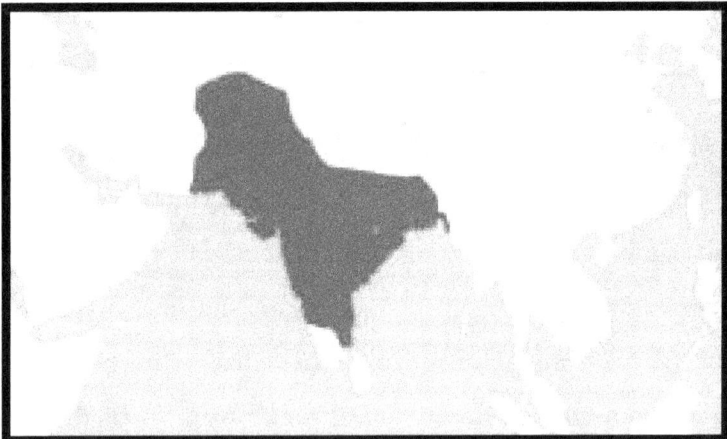

4.30 - Mughal Empire at its peak

Shah Jahan, the fifth emperor, erected historical monuments in India including the Taj Mahal at Agra, the Red Fort, and Jama Masjid at Delhi. The Taj Mahal was built as a monument to his wife, Mumtaz Mahal, who bore fourteen children and died during childbirth. Named a UNESCO World Heritage Site in 1983, the Taj Mahal is one of the finest examples of Mughal architecture.

4.31 - Taj Mahal, Agra

The Mughal Empire became well known in faraway lands. In Europe, the famous Italian composer and priest Antonio Vivaldi (1678–1741) composed and dedicated two concertos for strings, *Concerto Grosso Mogul* and *Il Gran Mogul*, to the Mughal Empire. It is unknown if these concertos, composed for Western instruments, were ever played for the Mughal emperors in India. After Aurangzeb, the empire was ruled by several kings and went into rapid decline.

1600–1947: BRITISH RAJ

The British did not come to India as invaders or conquerors; they came as traders. They formed the British East India Company in 1600 and set up a trading post in the west coast port of Surat in

David G. Mahal

1619. Later, the company opened trading stations at present-day Chennai, Mumbai, and Kolkata.

As the Mughal Empire dissolved, there were local wars for power. The British took advantage of these conflicts. In 1857, the last emperor of the Mughal Empire, Bahadur Shah II, was overthrown by the British and exiled to Burma (now Myanmar). The Mughal Empire was absorbed into the Indian Empire or the British Raj. After starting off as traders, they became conquerors and governors of the entire country. The British presence in India lasted more than three hundred years. They ruled India as a colony and left in 1947 after carving East Pakistan (now Bangladesh) and West Pakistan (now Pakistan) from Indian territory.

1602: ARRIVAL OF THE DUTCH

The Dutch in Travancore were the next to arrive. They established the Dutch East India Company in 1602 and trading outposts along the Indian coasts. The company eventually extended to Indonesia.

1674: ARRIVAL OF THE FRENCH

The French established outposts in Pondicherry (as seen in the Ang Lee film *Life of Pi*) and later in Chandernagore in Bengal, Yanam in Andhra Pradesh, Mahe, and Karaikal.

1799–1849: SIKH EMPIRE

Guru Nanak founded Sikhism in the fifteenth century, and his followers were called Sikhs. Their power continued to increase, and they became rulers of a large part of northwestern India. Maharaja Ranjit Singh was the famous ruler of the Sikh Empire. He modernized his infantry by employing officers from France, Italy, Greece, Russia, Germany, Austria, and England.[21]

At the time of his death, the empire covered areas of Punjab and present-day Kashmir and parts of northwestern India that are now in Pakistan. The Sikhs fought many successful battles with the British. After Ranjit Singh's death, the British were successful in taking over Punjab because of a disorganized Sikh army.

1942–1945: JAPANESE OCCUPATION

During World War II, the Japanese occupied the Andaman and Nicobar Islands in the Bay of Bengal, a part of Indian territory, for about three years.

INDIA: A GENETIC FOREST

Migrations and invasions are recurring themes in India's history. Over the years, so many different ethnic groups have arrived that the country has been aptly described as an "ethnological museum." The following is only a partial list of the ethnic groups that have come to India:

- Afghans
- Africans
- Arabs
- Armenians
- Aryans
- British
- Chinese
- Dutch
- French
- Greeks
- Huns
- Iranians
- Japanese
- Jews
- Kushans
- Mongols
- Parsees
- Persians
- Portuguese
- Scythians
- Syrians
- Tajiks
- Turks
- Uzbeks

During the convergence of ethnic groups, many migrants and invaders intermarried and mixed with the local people. This resulted in a highly mixed pool of foreign genes in India. Dr. B. S. Ahloowalia, author of *Invasion of the Genes*, explains it this way:

> "No other region ever experienced such traumatic changes and with such frequency as North India. The scale and frequency of the invasions was so huge and left such an immense impact on the introduction and spread of new genes, that the invasions can be rightly called gene invasions."[22]

CHAPTER 5

COUNTING RELATIVES

"It is likely that 80 percent of all marriages in history have been between second cousins or closer."—Robin Fox

Most of us know or remember our grandparents, and we may have heard the names of our great-grandparents. We may know where these relatives lived and what they did for a living. Because of better medical care, members of several generations may be living at the same time, but typically our knowledge about our family trees goes back only a few generations. Most of us know little or nothing about our earlier relatives, but the number of these earlier relatives is large, and the details may astound you. Population grows exponentially fast. If a woman's childbearing years are from sixteen to forty and she gives birth every two years, she can have twelve children. On average, six of these children will be girls, and they will grow up to be mothers. With each mother producing six more mothers, eight people can rapidly multiply into several million in a few hundred years. Assuming twenty-five years per generation, we find the following:

- One generation, or twenty-five years ago, you had two parents.

- Two generations, or fifty years ago, you had four grandparents.

- Three generations, or seventy-five years ago, you had eight great-grandparents.

Every generation has twice as many ancestors as the generation before. As shown in the family tree in chart 5.1 (which starts with the year 2000 for convenience), if you go back nine generations, or about two hundred years, more than five hundred people were responsible for your existence. Go back twenty generations, or about five hundred years, and there were more than a million ancestors. If you go back thirty generations, you'll find that you had well over one billion ancestors, nearly the current population of all India. Go back thirty-three generations, and the number of ancestors exceeds eight billion, more than the current population of the world. If you keep going back, eventually the answer exceeds the number of people who have ever lived on this planet. Obviously, this mathematical conclusion is incorrect. So what is going on?

The explanation is that many slots on a family tree are filled by the same people. A large number of ancestors are counted repeatedly,

Generations	Year	Ancestors
1	2000	2
2	1975	4
3	1950	8
4	1925	16
5	1900	32
6	1875	64
7	1850	128
8	1825	256
9	1800	512
10	1775	1,024
11	1750	2,048
12	1725	4,096
13	1700	8,192
14	1675	16,384
15	1650	32,768
16	1625	65,536
17	1600	131,072
18	1575	262,144
19	1550	524,288
20	1525	1,048,576
21	1500	2,097,152
22	1475	4,194,304
23	1450	8,388,608
24	1425	16,777,216
25	1400	33,554,432
26	1375	67,108,864
27	1350	134,217,728
28	1325	268,435,456
29	1300	536,870,912
30	1275	1,073,741,824
31	1250	2,147,483,648
32	1225	4,294,967,296
33	1200	8,589,934,592
34	1175	17,179,869,184
35	1150	34,359,738,368
36	1125	68,719,476,736
37	1100	137,438,953,472
38	1075	274,877,906,944
39	1050	549,755,813,888
40	1025	1,099,511,627,776
41	1000	2,199,023,255,552

5.1 - Family Tree

and there is a lot of duplication in the numbers. The actual number of ancestors in a family tree is far less than the mathematical answer, and you have "many" but not billions of distinct ancestors.

This phenomenon gets more pronounced the further back one goes, so a smaller proportion of one's family tree consists of "distinct" people with each generation. This type of reduction in the number of ancestors has a simple explanation.

PEDIGREE COLLAPSE

Normally, a person has eight great-grandparents. However, someone who marries his or her first cousin has only six individuals as great-grandparents, because two of them are duplicates. This type of reduction in the number of ancestors in a family tree is known as "pedigree collapse."

The primary reason for this phenomenon is that for much of history, many people stayed in the same place their entire lives. In historical communities that had no access to efficient transportation, sexual relationships and marriages most frequently took place between people living near each other, and spouses were often drawn from a pool of close relatives, sometimes from within the family.

English genealogist, physicist, and computer programmer Brian Pears says, "If every single marriage was between second cousins, then 30 generations ago [residents of Britain] would all have needed exactly 4,356,616 ancestors."[1] The mass movement of humans in the last few centuries has changed this phenomenon, and people tend to have far more diverse family trees than in the past. According to a recent survey, all Europeans living today are related to the same set of ancestors who lived one thousand years ago.[2]

Pedigree collapse occurs whenever one ancestor reproduces with someone to whom he or she is related. The numbers in chart 5.1 contain many ancestors who are duplicates and appear more than once. Looking back in one's family history, it is challenging to determine how many ancestors were real and how many were duplicates. The best we can do is estimate.

INCESTUOUS RELATIONSHIPS

Incest is defined as sexual activity among close family members. In the early stages of human evolution, this practice was probably common. Genetic studies of fossils from a cave in Siberia's Altai Mountains dated to about fifty thousand years ago have shown that inbreeding occurred among early humans.[3] In the past, royalty and nobility in many parts of the world (Egypt, Peru, Africa, Hawaii, and Thailand) were frequently required to marry their relatives. Egyptian pharaohs often married their sisters and, in some cases, their daughters.[4] Because they considered themselves descendants of gods, they did not want to mix their bloodlines with ordinary humans.

Such inbreeding has proved to be bad for the physical fitness of most species, and for humans, it has been banned in most societies. There are records of punishments and reprimands for inbreeding. King Suppiluliuma I of the Hittite Empire (1650–1200 BCE) warned one of his vassal rulers, "For Hatti it is an important custom that a brother does not have sex with his sister or female cousin. Whoever commits such an act is put to death. But your land is barbaric, for there a man regularly has sex with his sister or cousin…eat, drink, and be merry! But you must not desire to have sex with her."[5] Incest is no longer practiced among civilized humans, and it is illegal in most parts of the world, but it had an impact on pedigree collapse in the past.

CONSANGUINEOUS MARRIAGES

The word *consanguinity* comes from the Latin *con*, meaning shared, and *sanguis*, meaning blood. It describes a "shared blood" relationship. Marriage between people who have at least one recent common ancestor is known as consanguineous, and the children are considered inbred. The purpose of such a practice is usually to keep bonds, wealth, and property within a family.

Because of consanguineous marriages, Alfonso XIII, king of Spain, had ten great-great-grandparents instead of the usual sixteen. Alfonso XII had only eight great-great-grandparents in his official pedigree. Two of these great-great-grandparents, Charles IV of Spain and Maria Luisa of Parma, were parents of another twice great-grandmother, Maria Isabella of Spain. There is a long list of cousin marriages in the British monarchy. There are many other examples of royalty all over the world who married cousins.[6]

Consanguineous marriages have happened among commoners as well. Currently, couples related as second cousins or closer account for an estimated 10.4 percent of the global population with the highest rates in North and Sub-Saharan Africa, the Middle East, and West, Central, and South Asia.[7] In some tribes in the Amazon, it is customary for people to marry their first cousins. Even in nomadic societies like the ancestors of the Semitic people, marriage with a close cousin was prescribed. Cousin marriage is allowed in Islam, as written in the Quran.[8] The ideal marriage is between the children of two brothers, and this remains the norm in Arab and Muslim societies today.

In these circumstances, it's normal for people to have great-grandparents or great-great-grandparents who appear repeatedly in the pedigree tree. Researchers who study inbreeding track consanguineous marriages between second cousins or closer. In the following map (5.2), in Africa and the Middle East, 20 to more

113

David G. Mahal

than 50 percent of marriages fall into this category. Countries in Asia and South America report 1 to 10 percent consanguinity, and countries in Europe and North America, less than 1 percent. Data are unavailable for countries shown in white.

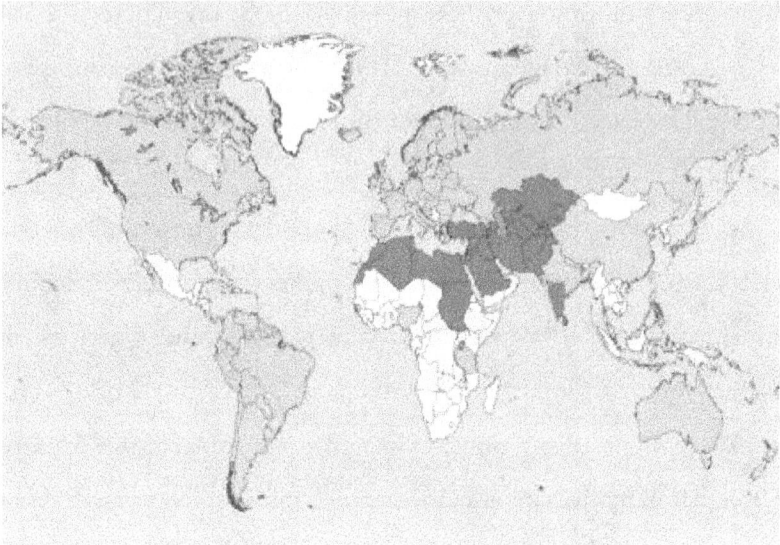

**5.2 - Consanguineous Marriages Worldwide
(Courtesy: Professor Alan Bittles)**

According to research by the Centre for Arab Genomic Studies in Dubai, at least half of all Gulf Arab marriages are between cousins with at least 35 percent of Qatari marriages between first cousins.

In Saudi Arabia, the number ranges from 25 to 42 percent, while in the United Arab Emirates, it is between 21 and 28 percent.[9] Research on other Arabic countries shows high levels of consanguinity.

About 70 percent of the nearly one million British Pakistanis are from the Mirpur region of Pakistan. The Mirpuri community emphasizes clan loyalty, or *biraderi*, and studies suggest that 60 percent of all Mirpuri marriages are to a first cousin with a substantial proportion of the remainder being between more distant relatives.[10] It is estimated that at least 55 percent of British Pakistanis are married to a first cousin.[11] According to Anne-Marie Nybo Andersen of South Danish University, in Pakistan, where cousin marriages have occurred for generations, the rate is about 70 percent.[12]

Consanguineous marriages continue all over the world. These are a few examples of prominent couplings:

- Albert Einstein, scientist, and his first cousin
- Charles Darwin, scientist, and his first cousin
- Edgar Allan Poe, author, and his cousin
- Edvard Grieg, composer, and his first cousin
- Eisaku Sato, prime minister of Japan, and his cousin
- Emperor Hirohito of Japan and his cousin
- Emperor Wu of Han and his cousin
- H. G. Wells, author, and his cousin
- Henry VIII of England and his near or distant cousins
- John Adams, second president of the United States, and his third cousin

David G. Mahal

- John F. Fitzgerald, grandfather of John F. Kennedy, and his second cousin
- Johann Sebastian Bach, composer, and his second cousin
- King Darius I of Persia and his cousin
- King Hussein of Jordan and his cousin
- Mao Zedong, founder of the People's Republic of China, and his second cousin
- Prithviraj Chauhan, a king in India, and his cousin
- Queen Victoria and Prince Albert
- Saddam Hussein and his first cousin
- Satyajit Ray, Indian filmmaker, and his first cousin

As shown in chart 5.3, this practice is prevalent in India as well. Based on a 2004–2005 survey conducted at the International Institute for Population Sciences in Mumbai, the South Indian states showed a greater occurrence of consanguineous marriages (Tamil Nadu at 38 percent) and North Indian states the lowest (Himachal Pradesh at 1 percent).[13]

Many countries have banned consanguineous marriages. Some religions prohibit such marriages as well. Still, it is estimated that about 20 percent of the human population lives in communities with a preference for consanguineous marriage and that at least 8.5 percent of children have consanguineous parents.[14] The family tree starts shrinking once you go back a few generations.[15]

States	% of Consanguinity	Sample Size
Tamil Nadu	38.0	306
Andhra Pradesh	29.6	346
Maharashtra	28.5	644
Karnataka	28.1	545
Jharkhand	12.2	97
Orissa	10.8	353
Uttar Pradesh	10.4	364
West Bengal	8.3	165
Bihar	6.5	187
Gujarat	6.3	212
Madhya Pradesh	5.4	353
Rajasthan	4.4	201
Northeast states	3.5	183
Kerala	3.2	261
Punjab	2.9	161
Haryana	2.3	273
Uttarakhand	1.3	47
Chhattisgarh	1.3	206
Assam	1.2	165
Himachal Pradesh	1.0	155
Total India	16.3	5,591

**5.3 - Consanguinity in India
(Source: IIPS, Mumbai)**

ENDOGAMY

Communication requires group members to speak the same language. There are more than five thousand languages spoken in the world, and there are about the same number of ethnic groups. Although there are about twenty main languages in India, the Indian Census of 1961 recorded a total of 1,652 "mother tongues," including distinct languages, dialects, and subdialects.[16] The speakers of these languages represent ethnic groups that are bound by their unique ties, values, and myths. The need for members of such ethnic groups to seek other people in their own group for friendship and marriage is natural and understandable.

Endogamy is the practice of marrying within a specific ethnic group, class, or social group. We can see this in most Indian matrimonial advertisements that specify that the spouse be from a certain religion or ethnic community. In countries like India with diverse ethnic communities, endogamous marriages have been the norm. Unless such marriages result in shared blood relationships, there is no duplication of ancestors in the family tree, but we can assume that some duplication exists.

POLYGAMY AND POLYANDRY

Polygamy means marriage to more than one woman. This practice has been common in many parts of the world and is still prevalent in some cultures. Polyandry means marriage to more than one man. As mentioned in the Mahabharata, Draupadi was married to the five Pandava brothers who were banished from their kingdom for thirteen years. At one time, this practice prevailed in parts of Himachal Pradesh and other regions of India. It is relatively rare today. Such marital practices do not have a significant impact on the family tree.

**5.4 - Draupadi with her five husbands
Dashavatara Temple, Deogarh**

THE REVISED FAMILY TREE

If we assume that 30 percent of the ancestors in each generation in the family tree shown in chart 5.1 are duplicates, we can make a simple mathematical adjustment. The revised chart 5.5 on the next page shows that the number of ancestors a thousand years ago even after a 30 percent reduction in each generation is well over one million. Of course, this is not a precise result. Suffice it to say that the number of our ancestors is very large.

According to the *Atlas of World Population History*, the estimated population of the Indian subcontinent in CE 1000 was about 80 million. As described in previous chapters, these people came from many different parts of the globe, intermingled, and multiplied. In a little over one thousand years this group mushroomed into a population of over one billion people. Our family trees emerge from the depths of this pool of humanity.

119

Generations	Year	Ancestors
1	2000	2
2	1975	3
3	1950	4
4	1925	5
5	1900	8
6	1875	11
7	1850	15
8	1825	21
9	1800	30
10	1775	41
11	1750	58
12	1725	81
13	1700	113
14	1675	159
15	1650	222
16	1625	311
17	1600	436
18	1575	610
19	1550	854
20	1525	1,195
21	1500	1,673
22	1475	2,343
23	1450	3,280
24	1425	4,592
25	1400	6,428
26	1375	9,000
27	1350	12,600
28	1325	17,640
29	1300	24,695
30	1275	34,573
31	1250	48,403
32	1225	67,764
33	1200	94,870
34	1175	132,817
35	1150	185,944
36	1125	260,322
37	1100	364,451
38	1075	510,232
39	1050	714,324
40	1025	1,000,054
41	1000	1,400,075

5.5 – Revised Family Tree

PART THREE

DNA SCIENCE

This part covers the science of genes and genealogy. It describes the Human Genome Project, which surveyed the genetic design of the human being. There are explanations about what genes are and how DNA analysis is used to more accurately trace ancestry. This part also includes a study of the DNA results of 1,291 individuals in fifty-two key ethnic communities from the Indian subcontinent. The results of the study identified eight major ancestral groups for this population.

CHAPTER 6

GENES AND GENEALOGY

"Without a doubt, this is the most important, most wondrous map ever produced by humankind."—Bill Clinton

In 1990, four-year-old Ashanti DeSilva of Indian heritage became the first person to receive gene therapy at the University of Southern California in Los Angeles. DeSilva suffered from a rare inherited immune disorder known as adenosine deaminase (ADA) deficiency that severely compromised her immune system. Without the enzyme that would protect her from bacteria and viruses, she was likely to die prematurely. She was injected with her own white blood cells that had been modified with a healthy version of her defective genes. Her treatment was a success, but gene therapy has had mixed results. In 1999, Jesse Gelsinger, an eighteen-year-old from Arizona, became the first patient to die from gene therapy rather than the disease he was suffering from.[1] There have been other cases where gene therapy did not work properly. Not all endeavors succeed immediately.

David G. Mahal

Scientists are working to translate the promise of gene therapy into treatments for a variety of medical conditions. For instance, medical practitioners are aware that a drug at the recommended standard dose does not work in the same manner for everyone. Researchers at the Mayo Clinic are studying how a patient's genes influence response to medicines. The goal is to deliver the right drug at the right dose and provide the best medical treatment based on a patient's specific genes.[2]

This knowledge about our genes is having profound impacts in the fields of medicine, biotechnology, the life sciences, forensics, and ancestry. It has become possible to study genes in depth only recently, and our grandparents could not have dreamed of such advances.

The Human Genome Project

Launched in 1990, the Human Genome Project (HGP) was a three billion-dollar joint project between the US Department of Energy and the National Institute of Health. The goal was to uncover the complete sequence of human DNA (genes are part of DNA). It became a massive international effort to determine the identity and location of nearly three billion molecules that make up human DNA. In 1998, Celera Genomics, a private, venture capital-funded company founded by Craig Venter, launched an effort to achieve the same goal. Because of such international efforts, the project was completed ahead of schedule.

On June 26, 2000, President Bill Clinton held a ceremony in the White House to celebrate the completion of the survey of the entire human genome. Tony Blair, the prime minister of England, joined him in this announcement via satellite. The results of the survey allowed researchers all over the world to begin to understand the internal blueprint of human beings. As our understanding of genetics, human diseases, and the aging process expands, it may be possible for people to regularly live one hundred years or more by the end of this century. This new science has also allowed us to explore our ancestry by analyzing our genes.

DNA AND ANCESTRY

The frozen, 5,300-year-old body of "Ötzi the Iceman" was found in the Italian Alps in 1991. It is reported that there are at least nineteen genetic relatives of Ötzi living in the Tyrol region of Austria today. Researchers found nineteen genetic matches by analyzing DNA records of 3,700 Austrian blood donors. Scientists expect to find more living relatives of Ötzi in the nearby Swiss and Italian Alps.[3] These results were accomplished through recent advances in DNA testing.

As discussed earlier, it is relatively simple to identify ancestors going back a few hundred years. Beyond that, the task is complicated, because for most of us, there is no documentation. Luckily, there are new methods for tracing our ancestry. Because we inherit our DNA from our parents, we can track the genes in our DNA back thousands of years and determine where our ancestors came from. Genetic tests allow us to trace the path of ancestors and find out who they were, where they lived, and how they dispersed throughout the world. We can learn how we came to be where we are today.

The science of genetic or DNA testing has evolved rapidly in recent years. These days, laboratories in many parts of the world routinely perform such tests (see the Resources section). To collect DNA, all that is usually needed is a sample from the mouth—a painless swab of the inside of the cheek or a small amount of saliva. The laboratories conduct the test and provide a written report. Some laboratories perform the test anonymously and post the results, which can be accessed only with a secret code, on their website.

It is unnecessary for the average person to become an expert in the science of DNA testing, but it is useful to know the basic terminology and understand how the tests are performed and interpreted. Let us briefly review how DNA can be used to trace ancestry.

THE HUMAN CELL

All living beings are made of cells, which are the building blocks of life. Invisible to our eyes, the human body contains fifty to one hundred trillion microscopic cells, which are the smallest units of living matter. There are many different types of cells: blood, muscle, brain, hair, skin, fat, and many others. Each type of cell has its own purpose. For example, the cells in our eyes control vision, and heart muscle cells control how the heart functions. Some cells, such as those in the hair and skin, replicate frequently. Others, such as those in the central nervous system (the brain), rarely reproduce.

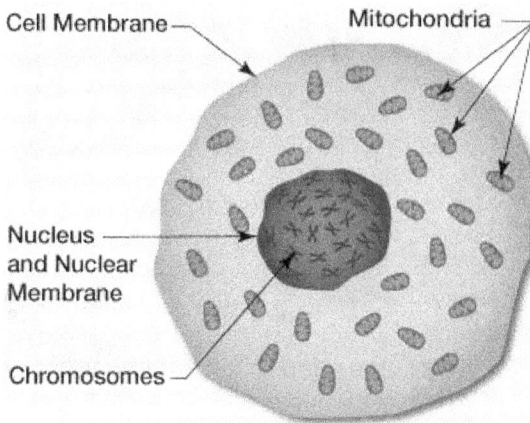

6.1 Human Cell (Courtesy: FamilyTreeDNA.com)

All cells have a similar structure. An outer membrane contains a nucleus that controls the cell and the nucleus has its own membrane. The "instructions" that tell the cell what to do reside in

David G. Mahal

the nucleus. These instructions are in the form of long, threadlike chemical molecules called chromosomes. Ordinarily, the chromosomes are loosely packed and not visible even under a microscope. They become visible only when the cell divides and replicates.

There are two types of chromosomes: X and Y. The nucleus of the cell for a female contains only X chromosomes, and the nucleus of the cell for a male contains both X and Y chromosomes.

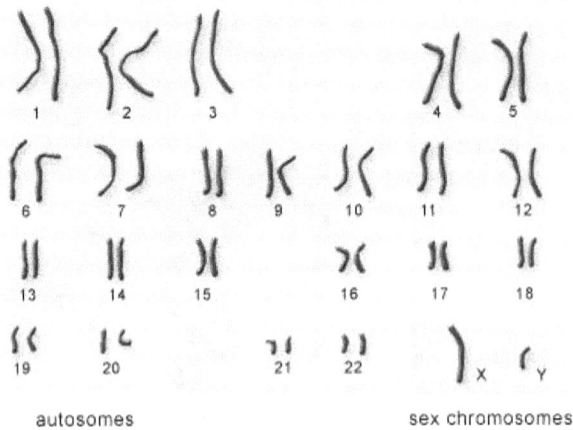

6.2 Autosomes and Sex Chromosomes
(Courtesy: US National Library of Medicine)

Each human cell contains forty-six chromosomes (X and Y) that are intertwined in twenty-three pairs. One member of each chromosome pair is inherited from the father and one is inherited from the mother. Of the twenty-three chromosome pairs, twenty-two pairs look the same in both males and females, and these are called autosomes. The twenty-third pair is different—it contains the sex chromosomes and differentiates males from females. If the X chromosome is inherited from the father with another X coming from the mother, the child is a female with two copies of the X chromosome (XX). If the Y chromosome is inherited from the father with the X coming from the mother, the child is a male with one X and one Y chromosome (XY). This is why it is said that the father determines the sex of a child.

DNA

DNA stands for deoxyribonucleic acid, and it carries all our genetic information. The chromosomes are made of strands of DNA. All the cells in the body, except red blood cells, contain a copy of the DNA, and nearly every cell has the same DNA. For all humans, 99.9 percent of DNA is identical, but the remaining 0.1 percent represents about three million differences between any two people. Therefore, except for identical twins, each person's DNA is unique. We are all similar and yet different. A short segment of DNA can serve as a "fingerprint" that is different for each person. This is how people are identified by using samples of their DNA.

The thin DNA strands in one cell can stretch to more than six feet (two meters) in length, and the entire DNA in the human body weighs about one-quarter of an ounce (about seven and a half grams). If the total DNA were placed end to end, it could theoretically stretch from the Earth to the Sun and back. The exact number of genes in the body is unknown, but the human genome contains the complete set of an estimated thirty thousand genes.

DNA located in the nucleus of the cell is called nuclear DNA or Y-DNA. A small amount of DNA is found outside the nucleus in the area known as the mitochondria, where it is called mitochondrial DNA or MT-DNA.

The Y chromosome (Y-DNA) is passed from father to son and unchanged from one generation to the next. It is passed down a male line and is unaffected by the X chromosome from the mother. The X chromosome (MT-DNA) is passed from mothers to their children, but only their daughters pass it on to the next generation. MT-DNA traces a maternal line. The Y-DNA is the only nuclear chromosome that escapes the reshuffling of parental genes during the reproduction process.

The DNA molecule is contained in two complementary chains that wrap around each other to resemble a twisted ladder or staircase known as the "double helix." The sides of the staircase are made of sugar and phosphate molecules. The stairs are made of nitrogen-containing chemicals called bases or nucleotides. Four different bases are present: adenine (A), thymine (T), cytosine (C), and guanine (G). The particular order of these four bases, called the DNA sequence or blueprint, guides protein production and how the cell functions.

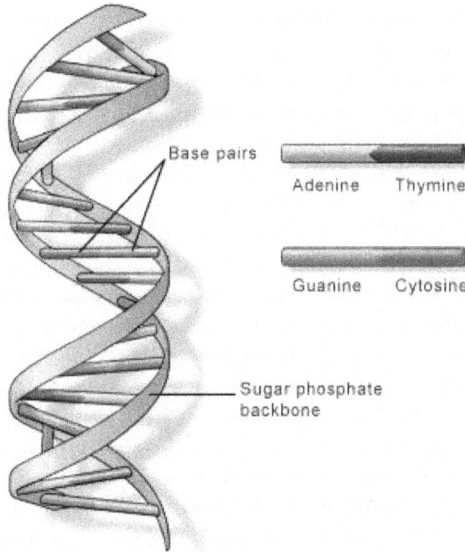

6.3 - Genes on DNA Strand
(Courtesy: US National Library of Medicine)

The four bases, also known as base pairs, always pair up in a set manner; A pairs with T, while C pairs with G. The DNA sequence consists of a large number of A, C, G, and T nucleotides. There are about three billion base pairs in the human genome. A portion of the DNA strands on the double helix may look like this:

Strand 1: A-C-T-C-G-G-T-A-A

Strand 2: T-G-A-G-C-C-A-T-T

David G. Mahal

When a cell divides for reproduction, the helix unwinds, splits down the middle, and copies itself to a new cell.

There is an ongoing daily molecular war in the nucleus of the human cell. DNA damage occurs at the rate of 20,000 lesions per cell per day.[4] This is caused by exposure to factors commonly found in food, water, air, and toxic materials, as well as byproducts of one's own metabolism. Most people ordinarily sustain these attacks and remain healthy; when they cannot they become sick.

GENES

The entire DNA strand does not contain genes. The genes are contained only on short sections of the DNA strands. Less than 2 percent of a person's total DNA represents genes, so there are long stretches of DNA between genes with no known function, and these are often referred to as "junk DNA."

Given any gene in the body, we can trace a single chain of ancestors back in time, following the lineage of this one gene. Because a typical organism is built from tens of thousands of genes, there are many ways to trace ancestry using this mechanism. This is done by analyzing markers and mutations in the DNA sequence.

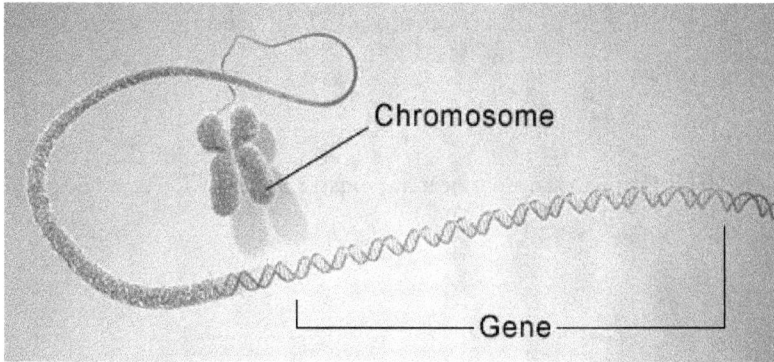

6.4 Genes on DNA Strand
(Courtesy: US National Library of Medicine)

MARKERS

A marker is a segment of the DNA that is associated with genetic characteristics. The markers are found at certain locations or *loci* (plural of *locus*, meaning place) on the chromosome where a base pattern is repeated a number of times. The terms *marker* and *locus* are often used interchangeably and can be confusing. For clarity, the marker is what is tested, and the locus is where the marker is located. Each marker is designated by a DYS number (D for DNA, Y for Y chromosome, S for segment) that is used to search for genetic matches. There is a known range of values for each marker.

The HUGO Gene Nomenclature Committee (HGNC) in Cambridge, England, is the worldwide authority that approves and assigns names and symbols for the human gene. The HGNC has

David G. Mahal

also assigned DYS numbers to the Y-STRs used in human genetic testing.

In the following example, the four-base pattern TCTA appears six times at marker DYS391:

TCTATCTATCTATCTATCTATCTA

The number of times a pattern is repeated is known as the number of repeats or the *allele* value for that marker. In this case, the allele value of marker DYS391 is six. Once markers are identified, they can be traced to their origin or the person called the "most recent common ancestor" of a group of individuals.

Two kinds of markers are used in genetic testing: short tandem repeats (STRs), and single nucleotide polymorphisms (SNPs). STRs and SNPs hold different types of information and are used for different purposes:

• STRs are found on the Y chromosome (Y-STRs) and used exclusively for tracing male lines of heredity.

• SNPs or "snips" are found on the Y chromosome and in MT-DNA. They are used for tracing male and female lines of heredity.

MUTATIONS

Where DNA is normally passed unchanged from parent to offspring, occasionally a random, naturally occurring, and usually harmless change occurs. Known as a mutation, the most common change occurs in a single base on the DNA sequence. For example, the base may change from a C to a G. There can be other changes such as the loss or addition of one or more bases. Although a mutation can change the instructions in a gene, most mutations have little or no impact.

Mutations can occur during a person's lifetime spontaneously or as the result of external factors such as radiation or exposure to certain viruses. Mutations occur at a low rate in every generation with about fifty changes in the billions of nucleotides in the human genome.[5] That amounts to about once every five hundred generations per marker.

The mutations serve as beacons. They can be mapped, because they are passed down through generations for thousands of years. When geneticists identify a mutation, they try to figure out when it first occurred and in which geographic region of the world. Each mutation is usually the beginning of a new lineage on a family tree and can trace ancestors to a specific time and place in history. By comparing the mutations in different people, geneticists can determine how closely they are related. By calculating the mutation

David G. Mahal

rate, they can also determine how long ago and where people split from their ancient clans.

HAPLOTYPE

A haplotype is the set of results for tested markers. DNA testing companies use different markers for producing their results and present them differently. The number of markers examined varies from one testing company to another, but most tests use from nine to forty markers.

In a nine-marker test, the probability that two people selected randomly will match each other on all nine markers is less than two in one thousand.[6]

The Genographic Project at the National Geographic Society uses the following twelve markers:

- DYS19
- DYS385a
- DYS385b
- DYS388
- DYS389-1
- DYS389-2
- DYS390
- DYS391
- DYS392
- DYS393
- DYS426
- DYS439

136

The common haplotype model used in Europe is called the Atlantic Modal Haplotype (AMH), and it uses six markers:

- DYS19
- DYS388
- DYS390
- DYS391
- DYS392
- DYS393

As an example, the typical results of a twelve-marker test for individual "A" may be presented as follows (the allele values appear under the DYS numbers).

Marker#	1	2	3	4	5	6	7	8	9	10	11	12
DYS #	19	389I	389II	390	391	392	393	385a	385b	426	439	388
A	14	12	29	22	10	11	12	15	18	10	13	14

To determine a genetic connection between individuals, the alleles are compared for each marker. The more alleles that match, the more likely it is that the individuals are related or have a common ancestor.

Here is a comparison of the test results for four individuals labeled A, B, C, and D.

Marker#	1	2	3	4	5	6	7	8	9	10	11	12
DYS #	19	389I	389II	390	391	392	393	385a	385b	426	439	388
A	15	13	29	22	11	14	12	10	16	10	12	16
B	16	13	29	24	11	14	13	11	14	11	10	14
C	16	13	29	25	10	14	13	11	14	11	10	14
D	14	13	29	22	11	11	12	15	18	10	13	14

David G. Mahal

The results show that B and C have matching alleles for all markers with only small differences for the values in DYS390 and DYS391. In terms of their ancient DNA, B and C are more closely related compared to A and B and have a common ancestor in the past.

HAPLOGROUP

Let us picture the entire human population as a large tree. A haplogroup is a branch of this tree, and a haplotype is a leaf on that branch. The haplogroup designates a cluster of people who have inherited common genetic markers from the same ancestor going back several thousand years. These designations allow genealogists to gain insights about direct paternal or maternal ancestors. The haplogroup is of primary interest to us in exploring our deep ancestry.

All humans belong to haplogroups which are designated according to their Y-DNA and MT-DNA. The haplogroup for any person is determined with data from a haplotype by using a computational model or software.

The haplogroups contain many branches called subhaplogroups or subclades. The top-level haplogroups are expressed in letters (A, B, C, and so on). Their subhaplogroups or subclades are expressed in letters and numbers (G2, R1b1, E3b1b, and so on).

THE PHYLOGENETIC TREE

Phylogeography is the science of determining the place of origin and spread of genetic lineages. It involves the study of processes that may be responsible for the geographic distribution of human beings. It uses markers to assign people who share a set of genetic markers and therefore share an ancestor to their respective haplogroup.

The International Society of Genetic Geology (ISOGG) maintains a detailed Y-DNA phylogenetic tree of mankind. There is a similar tree based on MT-DNA maintained at Erasmus MC in The Netherlands. The trees are updated as new data become available.

A shortened version of the Y-DNA tree appears in chart 6.5. It shows the key markers such as M9 and M20 on the left side. The twenty top-level haplogroups from A to T appear on the right side.

DNA TESTS

Although several different tests are used in DNA studies, there are only two of interest for our purposes: Y-DNA and MT-DNA.

• Y-DNA tests are available only to males, because the genes are passed from father to son. The tests examine either STRs or SNPs on the Y chromosome, and they provide a haplotype that is

David G. Mahal

used to predict the haplogroup. Of the two tests, the SNP test is more precise.

•   MT-DNA tests are available to both males and females. The tests examine matrilineal ancestry using the DNA in the mitochondria.

Because paternity cannot be determined for females through Y-DNA tests, a close male family member (father or brother) can be tested to determine deep ancestry.

WHAT DNA TESTS DO NOT TELL US

The tests do not produce a family tree. They cannot tell who one's great-great-great-grandfather was or which town or village he came from. The tests can tell if two people are related but cannot determine the degree of relationship (for example, if they are first cousins or fifth cousins). The tests can reveal information only about a small percentage of the genome.

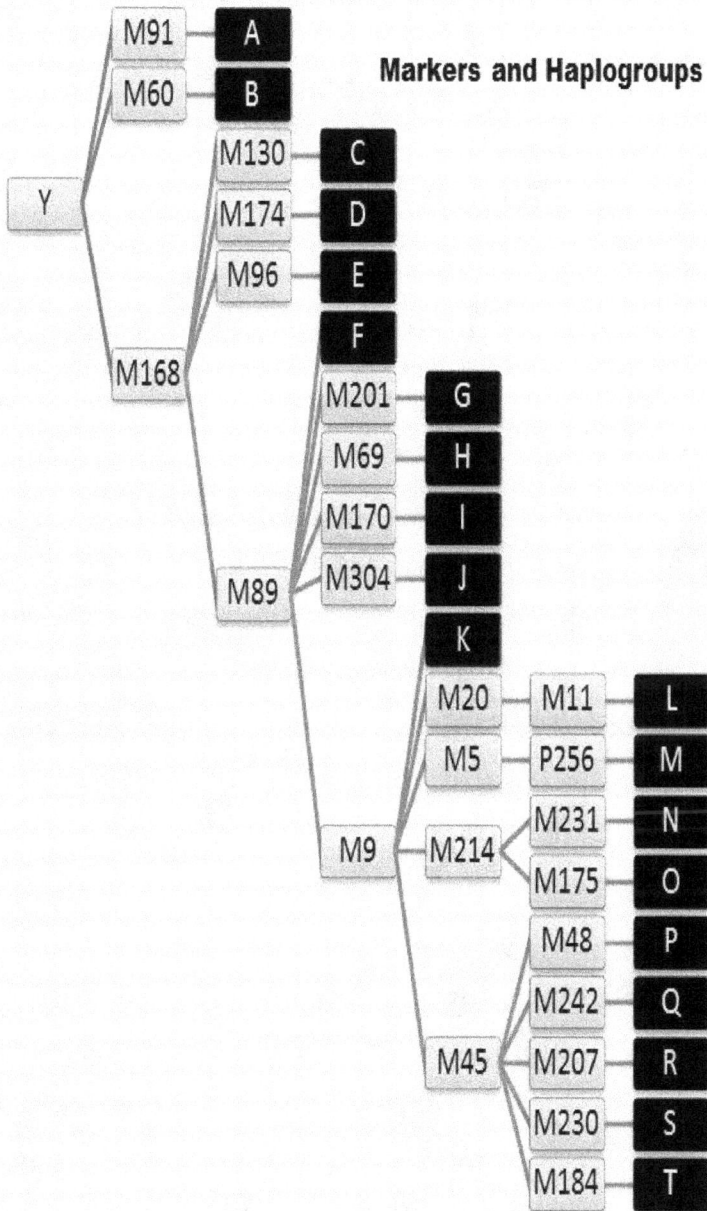

Markers and Haplogroups

6.5 Y-DNA Phylogenetic Tree

CHAPTER 7

THE ANCESTORS

"Written records go back to the dawn of written history. DNA goes back to the dawn of human existence."—George Church

As discussed earlier, all people living today are genetically connected to a man who lived in Africa more than one hundred thousand years ago. This great ancestor is often termed the "Y-chromosomal Adam." Descendants of this man from the present-day region of Ethiopia dispersed in different directions. Some stayed in Africa and moved to different parts of the region, and others shifted to the Arabian Peninsula and began their journeys to other lands.

One group from the Arabian Peninsula took the coastal route through India, Myanmar, and Malaysia to Australia. Another group moved north into central Asia and eventually toward China, Siberia, and Europe. A related group went west toward the Mediterranean and Europe. All these journeys were undertaken on foot, possibly with the help of some animals after they were domesticated. There is no evidence of ocean sailing technology that long ago.

These migrations did not occur in straight lines. People moved to a new area and stayed there, continued onward and dispersed in different directions, or returned to an earlier area. By living in different climates, eating different types of food, and breeding with people who were already there, the color, size, and physiognomy changed among the groups. As we have seen, many migrations into the Indian subcontinent were peaceful, and many were extremely violent. The ancestors come from this large pool of people and they are identified by their haplogroups.

MAJOR INDIAN HAPLOGROUPS

Although there are twenty major Y-DNA haplogroups (designated with the letters A to T), not all of them are observed in the Indian subcontinent in significant numbers. For example, haplogroups A and B are primarily seen in Africa. Haplogroup A is believed to be the original haplogroup of the Y-chromosomal Adam. Similarly, there are haplogroups that are more prevalent in other parts of the world. A few haplogroups are prominent only in Europe. For example, haplogroup I and its subgroups are predominantly found in northwestern Europe, and haplogroup N is predominantly found in northeastern Europe. Although haplogroup Q is primarily associated with Native American populations, with the

David G. Mahal

vast immigrations that have taken place over the years, North America now has a wide representation of different haplogroups.[1]

A comprehensive Y-Chromosome Haplotype Reference Database (YHRD) is maintained at YHRD.org in Berlin. As of this writing, laboratories and institutions from around the world have contributed over 130,000 haplotypes of different population groups for this database. For the purposes of our study, 1,291 haplotypes from this database were analyzed, representing fifty-two different ethnic communities. Of these, twenty-nine communities were in India, fourteen in Pakistan, three each in Bangladesh and the United Kingdom, and one each in Singapore, Malaysia, and Sri Lanka. All people in the communities outside India were originally of Indian or Pakistani origin.

Sample Population (n=1,291)		
Country	n	%
India	689	53.4%
Pakistan	422	32.7%
Bangladesh	62	4.8%
United Kingdom	53	4.1%
Malaysia	27	2.1%
Sri Lanka	20	1.5%
Singapore	18	1.4%
Total	1,291	100.0%

7.1 Population Sample Used

All haplotypes in the sample population were processed through Whit Athey's Haplogroup Predictor, a software program, and the results were sorted and graphed in Excel. Only the predominant top-level haplogroups were identified. The subhaplogroups or subclades were not used. All outcomes are for male paternal lines.

The results are rough approximations of what would be found in the total population of the communities. The samples for some communities (e.g., Sri Lanka, Singapore) are small and only serve as indicators. The results do not include all ethnic communities of the Indian subcontinent, and do not represent the entire population of the land.

Of the twenty major haplogroups, the following eight were identified as having significant representation in the sample population. Four other haplogroups—C, O, N, and T—represent a small portion of the sample population and appear under Miscellaneous. The overall distribution is illustrated in chart 7-2.

- E
- G
- H
- I

- J
- L
- Q
- R

Charts 7.3 to 7.6 show how the ethnic communities in our sample population are represented in these haplogroups.

David G. Mahal

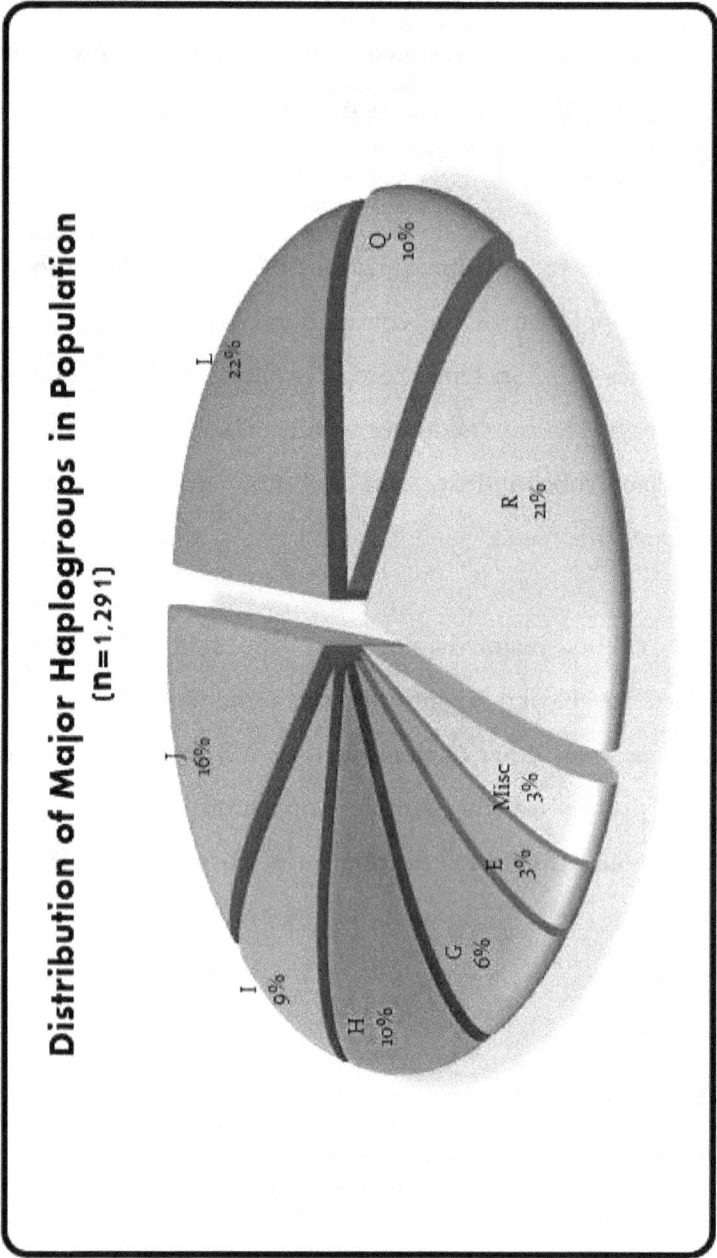

Distribution of Major Haplogroups in Population
(n=1,291)

I 22%
Q 10%
R 21%
Misc 3%
E 3%
G 6%
J 16%
I 9%
H 10%

7.2 - Distribution of Haplogroups

146

Represented Communities in India (n=689)

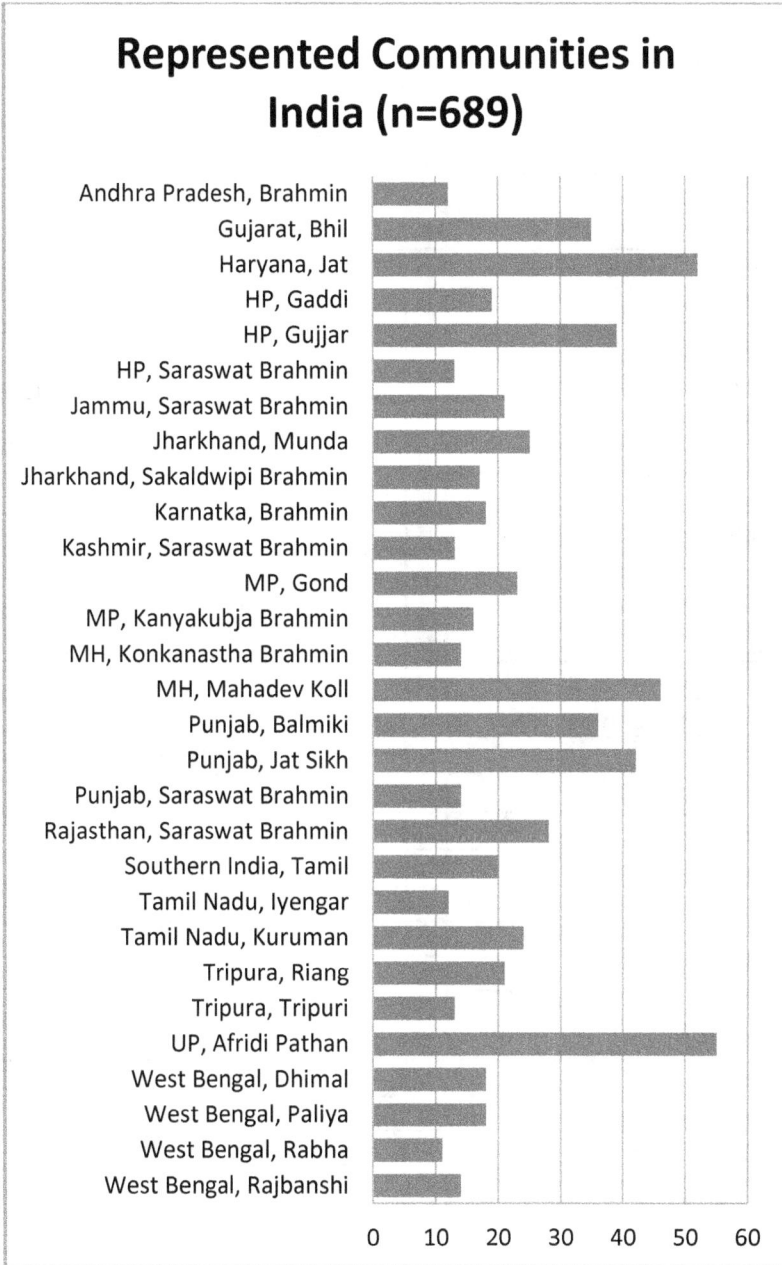

Andhra Pradesh, Brahmin	
Gujarat, Bhil	
Haryana, Jat	
HP, Gaddi	
HP, Gujjar	
HP, Saraswat Brahmin	
Jammu, Saraswat Brahmin	
Jharkhand, Munda	
Jharkhand, Sakaldwipi Brahmin	
Karnatka, Brahmin	
Kashmir, Saraswat Brahmin	
MP, Gond	
MP, Kanyakubja Brahmin	
MH, Konkanastha Brahmin	
MH, Mahadev Koll	
Punjab, Balmiki	
Punjab, Jat Sikh	
Punjab, Saraswat Brahmin	
Rajasthan, Saraswat Brahmin	
Southern India, Tamil	
Tamil Nadu, Iyengar	
Tamil Nadu, Kuruman	
Tripura, Riang	
Tripura, Tripuri	
UP, Afridi Pathan	
West Bengal, Dhimal	
West Bengal, Paliya	
West Bengal, Rabha	
West Bengal, Rajbanshi	

HP = Himachal Pradesh, MH = Maharashtra, MP = Madhya Pradesh, UP = Uttar Pradesh

7.3 - Population Sample: India

147

David G. Mahal

INDIA: REPRESENTATION IN MAJOR HAPLOGROUPS (n=689)											
Community	n	C	E	G	H	I	J	L	O	Q	R
Andhra Pradesh, Brahmin	12		√					√			√
Gujarat, Bhil	35			√	√	√	√	√		√	√
Haryana, Jat	52			√			√	√		√	√
Himachal Pradesh, Saraswat Brahmin	13						√	√		√	√
Himachal Pradesh, Gujjar	39				√		√				√
Himacha Pradesh, Gaddi	19			√	√		√				√
Jharkhand, Sakaldwipi Brahmin	17	√			√						√
Jharkhand, Munda	25				√	√			√		
Jammu, Saraswat Brahmin	21				√		√	√		√	√
Karnatka, Brahmin	18		√			√	√	√		√	√
Kashmir, Saraswat Brahmin	13				√		√	√		√	
Madhya Pradesh, Kanyakubja Brahmin	16			√	√		√			√	√
Madhya Pradesh, Gond	23			√	√			√			√
Maharashtra, Konkanastha Brahmin	14		√				√	√		√	√
Maharashtra, Mahadev Koll	46		√		√	√	√	√			
Punjab, Saraswat Brahmin	14				√		√	√		√	√
Punjab, Jat Sikh	42		√				√	√		√	√
Punjab, Balmiki	36				√		√	√		√	
Rajasthan, Saraswat Brahmin	28				√		√	√			√
Southern India, Tamil	20		√	√	√		√	√		√	
Tamil Nadu, Iyengar	12						√	√			√
Tamil Nadu, Kuruman	24			√	√	√	√	√		√	
Tripura, Riang	21				√		√	√		√	√
India, Tripura, Tripuri	13						√	√		√	
Uttar Pradesh, Afridi Pathan	55		√	√		√	√	√			√
West Bengal, Dhimal	18					√	√	√		√	
West Bengal, Paliya	18						√	√			√
West Bengal, Rabha	11							√		√	√
West Bengal, Rajbanshi	14						√	√		√	√
Total	689	0%	2%	7%	13%	3%	13%	26%	3%	13%	19%

7.4 - Major Haplogroups, India

148

Represented Communities in Other Countries (n=602)

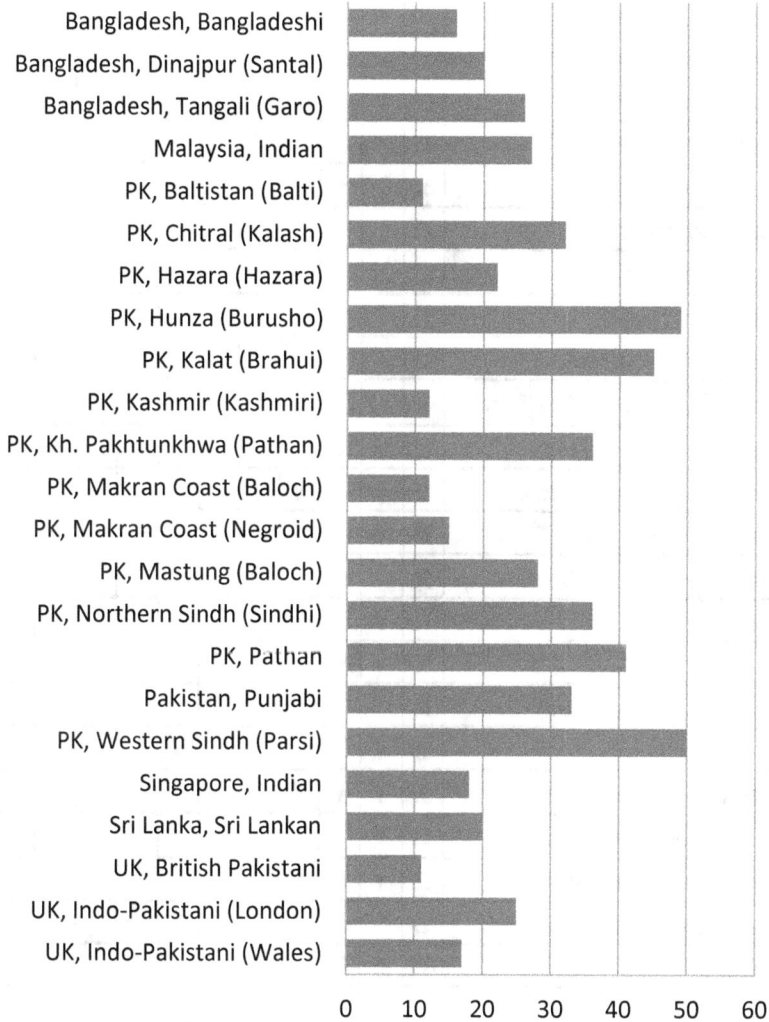

Chart with horizontal bars for the following communities:

- Bangladesh, Bangladeshi
- Bangladesh, Dinajpur (Santal)
- Bangladesh, Tangali (Garo)
- Malaysia, Indian
- PK, Baltistan (Balti)
- PK, Chitral (Kalash)
- PK, Hazara (Hazara)
- PK, Hunza (Burusho)
- PK, Kalat (Brahui)
- PK, Kashmir (Kashmiri)
- PK, Kh. Pakhtunkhwa (Pathan)
- PK, Makran Coast (Baloch)
- PK, Makran Coast (Negroid)
- PK, Mastung (Baloch)
- PK, Northern Sindh (Sindhi)
- PK, Pathan
- Pakistan, Punjabi
- PK, Western Sindh (Parsi)
- Singapore, Indian
- Sri Lanka, Sri Lankan
- UK, British Pakistani
- UK, Indo-Pakistani (London)
- UK, Indo-Pakistani (Wales)

0   10   20   30   40   50   60

PK = Pakistan, UK = United Kingdom

7.5 - Population Sample: Other Countries

OTHER COUNTRIES : REPRESENTATION IN MAJOR HAPLOGROUPS (n=602)											
Community	n	E	G	H	I	J	L	N	Q	R	T
Bangladesh, Bangladeshi	16			√		√	√		√	√	
Bangladesh, Dinajpur (Santal)	20			√	√				√		√
Bangladesh, Tangali (Garo)	26					√	√		√		√
Malaysia, Indian	27	√	√	√		√	√			√	
Pakistan, Baltistan (Balti)	11				√	√				√	√
Pakistan, Chitral (Kalash)	32		√	√	√	√	√	√			
Pakistan, Hazara (Hazara)	22				√			√	√	√	√
Pakistan, Hunza (Burusho)	49			√	√	√	√		√	√	
Pakistan, Kalat (Brahui)	45		√		√	√				√	
Pakistan, Kashmir (Kashmiri)	12					√				√	
Pakistan, Khyber Pakhtunkhwa (Pathan)	36					√	√			√	
Pakistan, Makran Coast (Baloch)	12	√	√		√	√	√			√	
Pakistan, Makran Coast (Negroid)	15	√		√	√	√			√	√	
Pakistan, Mastung (Baloch)	28	√			√	√	√			√	
Pakistan, Northern Sindh (Sindhi)	36				√	√	√	√		√	
Pakistan, Pathan	41	√			√		√			√	√
Pakistan, Punjabi	33	√	√			√	√			√	
Pakistan, Western Sindh (Parsi)	50				√	√	√			√	√
Singapore, Indian	18	√			√	√	√		√	√	
Sri Lanka, Sri Lankan	20	√	√	√			√			√	√
United Kingdom, British Pakistani	11	√		√		√	√		√		
United Kingdom, Indo-Pakistani London	25	√		√	√	√	√		√	√	
United Kingdom, Indo-Pakistani Wales	17			√			√			√	
Total	602	3%	5%	6%	14%	19%	18%	1%	6%	24%	2%

7.6 - Major Haplogroups, Other Countries

SUMMARY

There is no community in our sample that belongs to a single haplogroup and that would indicate one distant ancestor for all of its members. In other words, there is no community with a pure bloodline that can be traced to a single common ancestral group.

Every community represented in the sample has members that belong to more than one haplogroup, indicating that the community's members have different lines of ancestors. For example, the Saraswat Brahmins of Punjab have members that belong to haplogroups H, J, Q, R, and L, indicating at least five different lines of ancestors. Similarly, the Jats (my ethnic group), from Punjab and Haryana, have members in haplogroups E, G, J, L, Q, and R, indicating at least six different ancestral lines. As another example, the Kashmiri community in Pakistan has members in only two haplogroups, J and R, indicating possibly only two separate lines of ancestry.

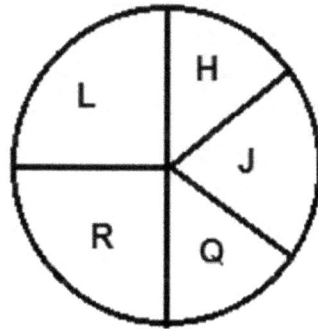

4.7 – Community with Members in Five Haplogroups

At the same time, many members from different ethnic communities belong to the same haplogroup, and share the same

David G. Mahal

common ancestor. For example, as shown in figure 7.8, both groups 1 and 2 have some members in the same haplogroup R.

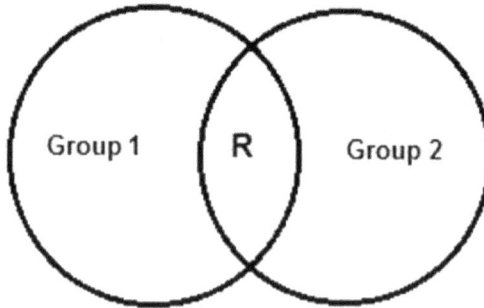

7.8 Two Groups with Members in Haplogroup R

By reviewing charts 7.4 and 7.6, you will see that forty one of the fifty-two communities in our sample have members in the haplogroup L. Similarly, thirteen of the fifty-two communities have members in the haplogroup G. There are other examples. The key point is that irrespective of which ethnic community they belong to all members of the same haplogroup have the same common ancestral line.

It may be difficult for some people to accept that, for example, some Bangladeshis, Balochs, Brahmins, Bhils, Balmikis, Jats, Pathans, Sindhis, and Parsis belong to the same haplogroup and have the same common ancestor in the distant past. But this is a fact and it is based on DNA evidence.

CHAPTER 8

MAJOR HAPLOGROUPS

"The greatest history book ever written is the one hidden in our DNA."—Spencer Wells

The eight major Y-DNA haplogroups identified in our study are described in more detail in the following pages. A chart for each haplogroup shows the countries represented in the sample. The symbol *n* represents the number of people. The haplogroup's ancestral line on the phylogenetic tree is identified. There is a brief description of where the haplogroup originated. Another chart shows the top ten ethnic communities with the highest representation in the haplogroup in their sample population. The details for each ethnic community are provided in the Appendix.

The ancestral line for each haplogroup can be traced on the phylogenetic tree provided in chapter 6. The age of the M168 mutation on the phylogenetic tree has been estimated to be forty thousand years, and it represents the last ancestor of all non-African Y chromosomes.[1]

David G. Mahal

HAPLOGROUP E

Ancestral Line on Phylogenetic Tree: M168 → M96

This haplogroup originated in northeast Africa some thirty to forty thousand years ago. The group is found in all regions in Africa and exists in some populations in the Middle East, Europe, and Asia. One of its subclades that may have evolved in the Middle East is predominantly found along the Mediterranean coast.

Members of this group may have emerged from what is known as the "Middle East clan." The group is also present in North America primarily due to the slave trade that brought Africans to America.

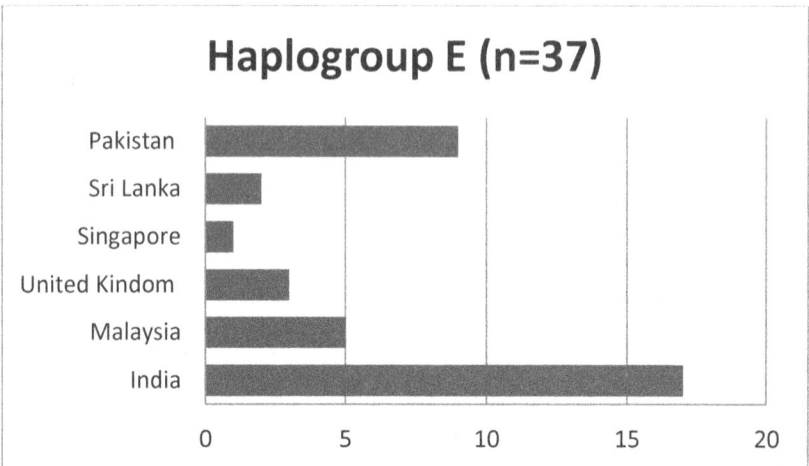

8.1 - Geographical Representation for E

Major Communities in E

Malaysia, Indian	
United Kingdom, British Pakistani (Wales)	
Andhra Pradesh, Brahmin	
Southern India, Tamil	
Maharashtra, Konkanastha Brahmin	
Pakistan, Makran Coast (Negroid)	
Maharashtra, Mahadev Koll	
Sri Lanka, Sri Lankan	
Pakistan, Makran Coast (Baloch)	
Pakistan, Mastung (Baloch)	

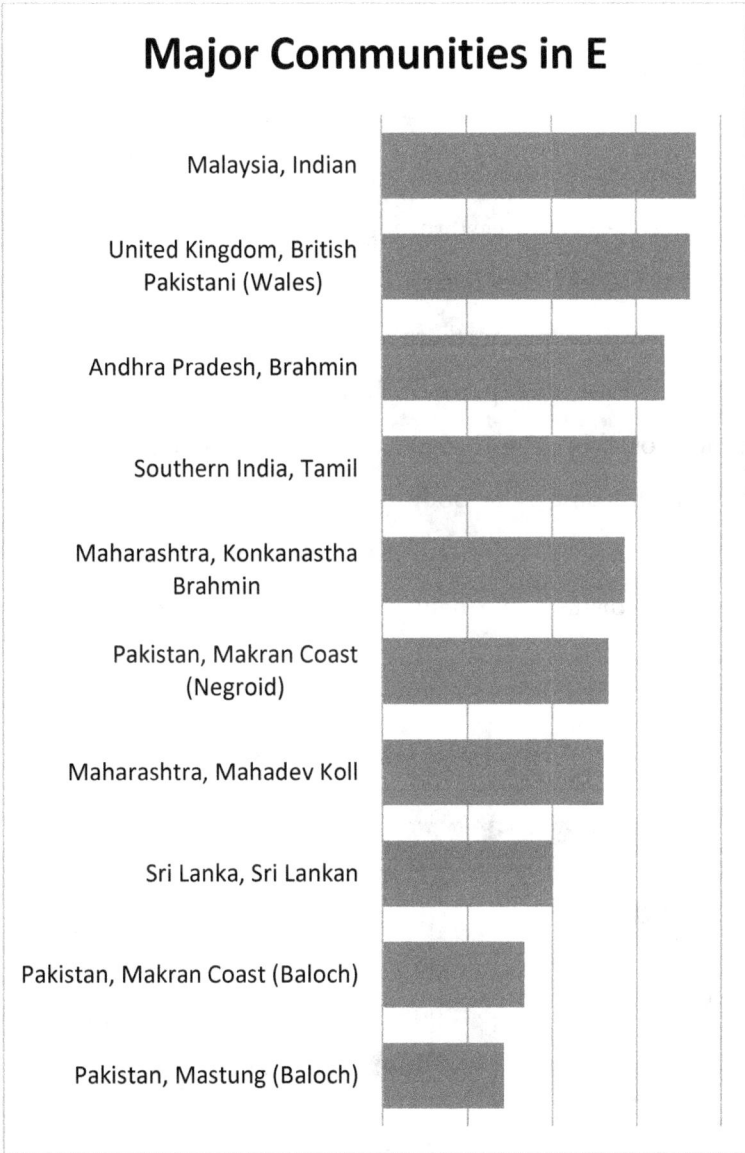

8.2 - Community Representation in E

David G. Mahal

HAPLOGROUP G

Ancestral Line on Phylogenetic Tree: M168 → M89 → M201

The M201 marker emerged about thirty thousand years ago somewhere along the eastern edge of the Middle East or in the Himalayan foothills of Pakistan or India. This haplogroup is widely distributed in Europe, northern and western Asia, northern Africa, the Middle East, and parts of India. There are indications that members of this group were engaged in farming in the Indus Valley at one time. The body of Ötzi the Iceman found in the Italian Alps in 1991 belongs to a subclade of this group. Another subclade is a distinctive genetic marker of Ashkenazi Jews.

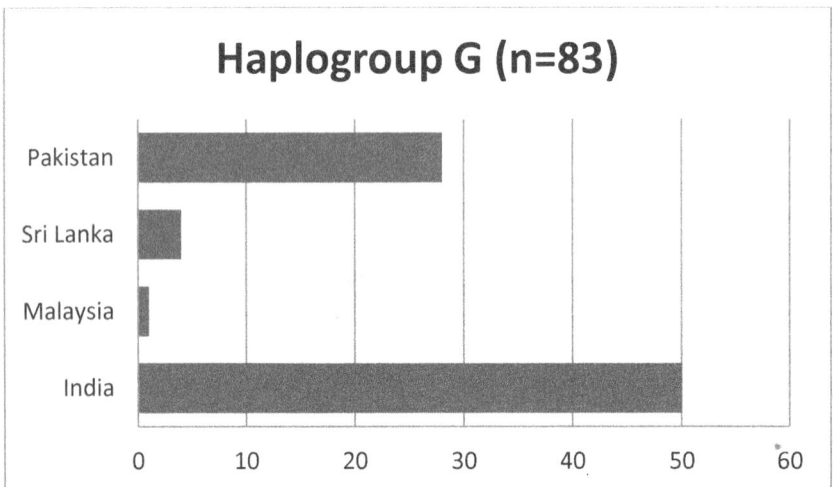

Haplogroup G (n=83)

8.3 - Geographical Representation for G

156

In a 2010 study of forty-five Cochin Jews from South India, it was found that none belonged to this group, but 6.5 percent of thirty-one Bene Israel Jews from Mumbai were in this group.[2]

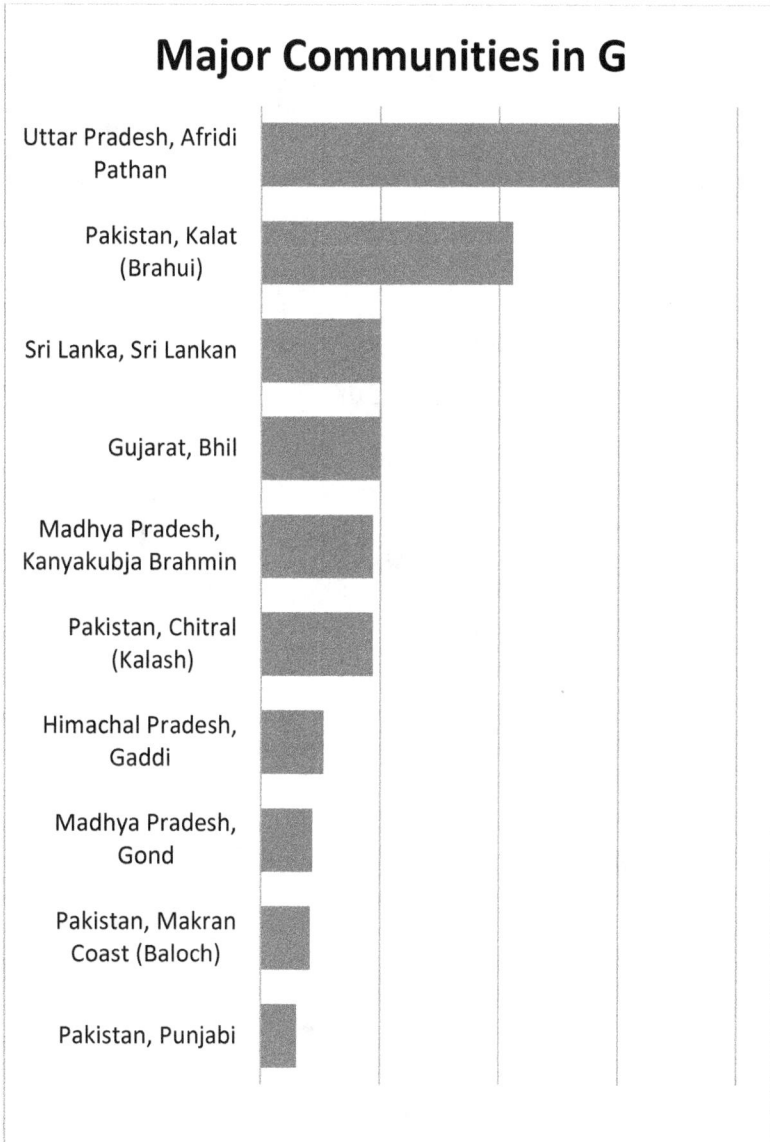

Major Communities in G

Uttar Pradesh, Afridi Pathan	
Pakistan, Kalat (Brahui)	
Sri Lanka, Sri Lankan	
Gujarat, Bhil	
Madhya Pradesh, Kanyakubja Brahmin	
Pakistan, Chitral (Kalash)	
Himachal Pradesh, Gaddi	
Madhya Pradesh, Gond	
Pakistan, Makran Coast (Baloch)	
Pakistan, Punjabi	

8.4 - Community Representation in G

David G. Mahal

HAPLOGROUP H

Ancestral Line on Phylogenetic Tree: M168 → M89 → M69

This haplogroup has a large representation in the Indian subcontinent and can be referred to as the "Indian haplogroup." Originally from Iran or the Middle East, marker M69 originated in western India about thirty thousand years ago. This group is considered to be part of a second wave of migrations to India. The Romany people, also known as gypsies and believed to originate from India, belong to a subclade of this group.

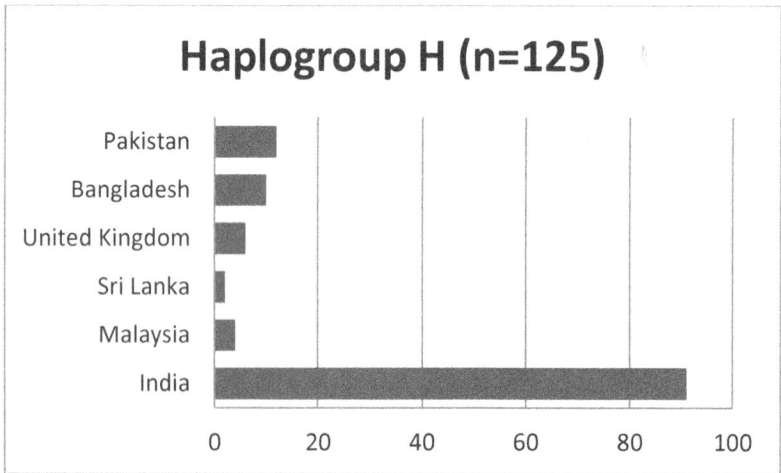

Haplogroup H (n=125)

Pakistan, Bangladesh, United Kingdom, Sri Lanka, Malaysia, India

0 20 40 60 80 100

8.5 - Geographical Representation for H

Major Communities in H

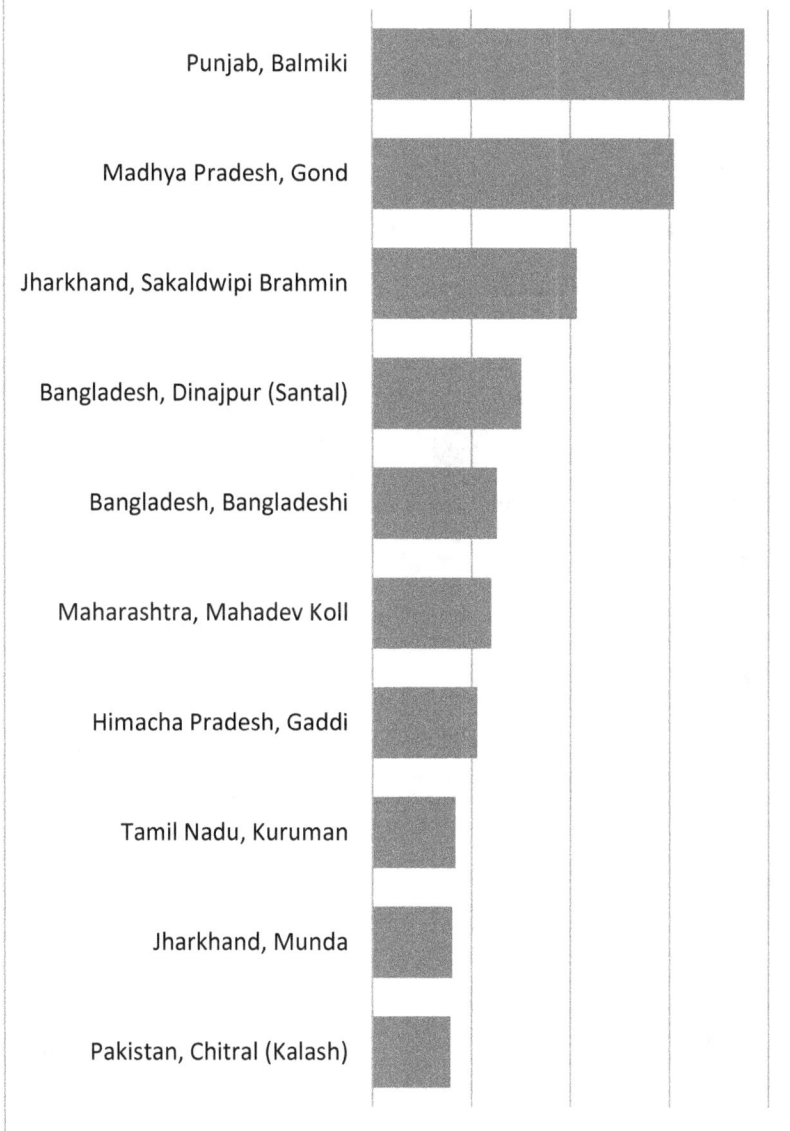

Punjab, Balmiki	
Madhya Pradesh, Gond	
Jharkhand, Sakaldwipi Brahmin	
Bangladesh, Dinajpur (Santal)	
Bangladesh, Bangladeshi	
Maharashtra, Mahadev Koll	
Himacha Pradesh, Gaddi	
Tamil Nadu, Kuruman	
Jharkhand, Munda	
Pakistan, Chitral (Kalash)	

8.6 - Community Representation in H

David G. Mahal

HAPLOGROUP I

Ancestral Line on Phylogenetic Tree: M168 → M89 → M170

This is predominantly a European haplogroup, and it dates to about twenty-five thousand years ago. Its subclades are widespread in the Balkans, Spain, France, and central and northwestern Europe with high frequencies in Scandinavian populations of Swedish and Norwegian lineages (e.g., the Vikings). There is a small representation in the Near East and central Asia. The Indian and Pakistani lineages emerged from these geographical areas. The highest represented ethnic communities in the sample population are primarily from Pakistan.

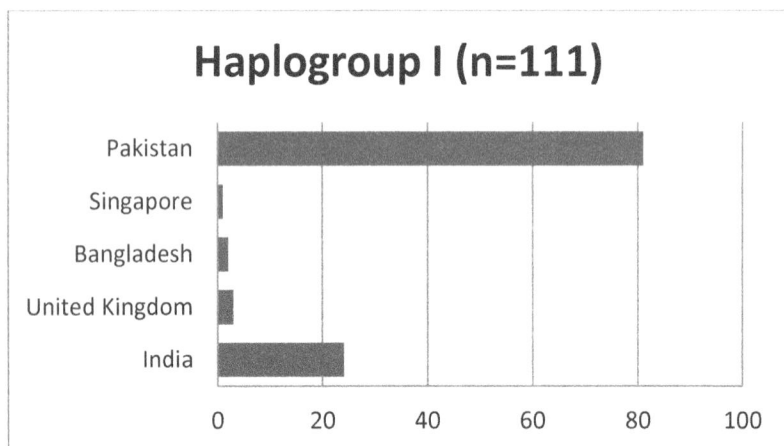

8.7 - Geographical Representation for I

Major Communities in I

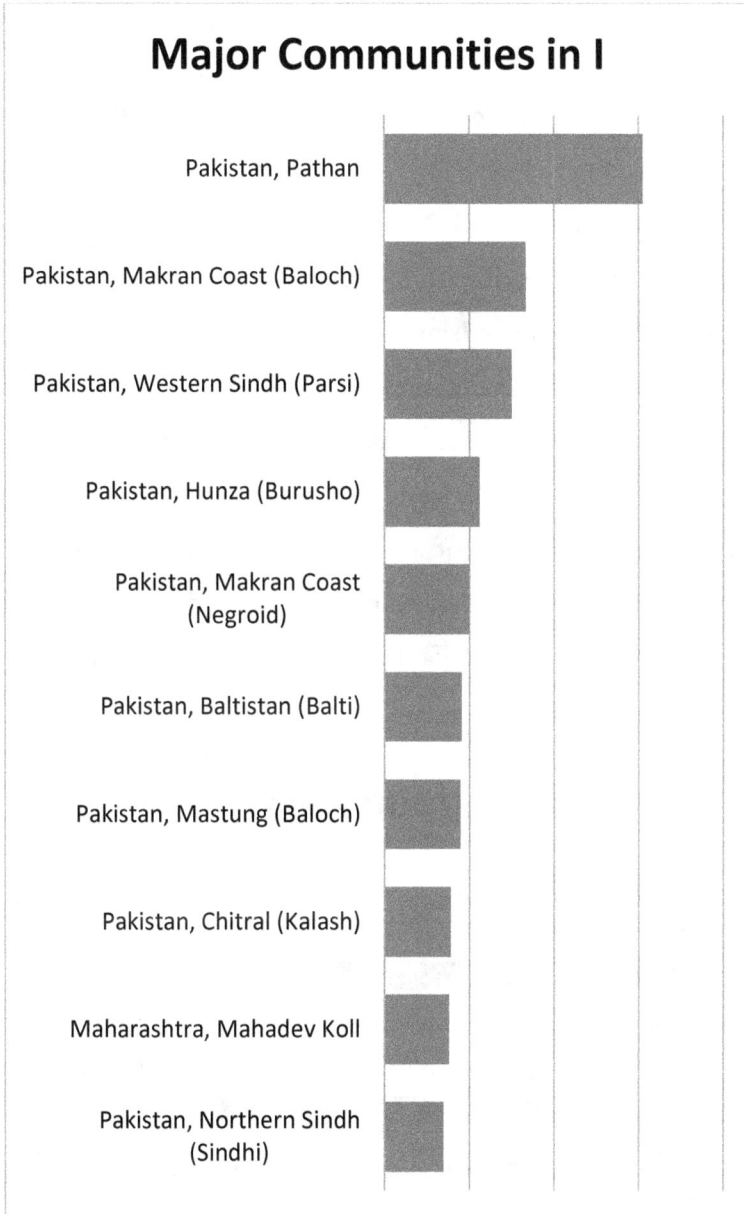

Pakistan, Pathan
Pakistan, Makran Coast (Baloch)
Pakistan, Western Sindh (Parsi)
Pakistan, Hunza (Burusho)
Pakistan, Makran Coast (Negroid)
Pakistan, Baltistan (Balti)
Pakistan, Mastung (Baloch)
Pakistan, Chitral (Kalash)
Maharashtra, Mahadev Koll
Pakistan, Northern Sindh (Sindhi)

8.8 - Community Representation in I

David G. Mahal

HAPLOGROUP J

Ancestral Line on Phylogenetic Tree: M168 → M89 → M304

The man carrying the M304 mutation was born around fifteen thousand years ago in the Middle East area known as the Fertile Crescent, which includes Israel, the West Bank, Jordan, Lebanon, Syria, and Iraq. There is a dominant Arabic lineage. This group and its subclades are found predominantly around the coast of the Mediterranean, the Middle East, North Africa, and Ethiopia. One subclade has a frequency of about 30 percent among the Jewish people. Middle Eastern traders carried this marker into regions including Europe, central Asia, India, and Pakistan.[3]

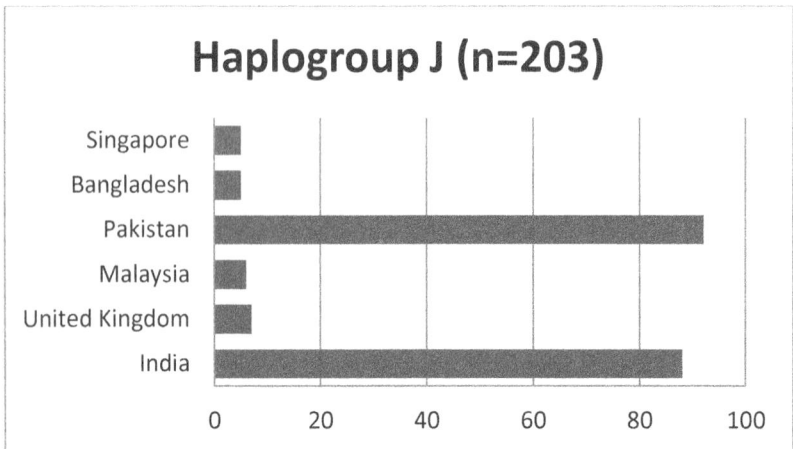

8.9 - Geographical Representation for J

162

Major Communities in J

Pakistan, Punjabi	
Rajasthan, Saraswat Brahmin	
Pakistan, Kalat (Brahui)	
Pakistan, Western Sindh (Parsi)	
UK, British Pakistani (Wales)	
Gujarat, Bhil	
West Bengal, Dhimal	
Tripura, Riang	
Singapore, Indian	
Pakistan, Kashmir (Kashmiri)	

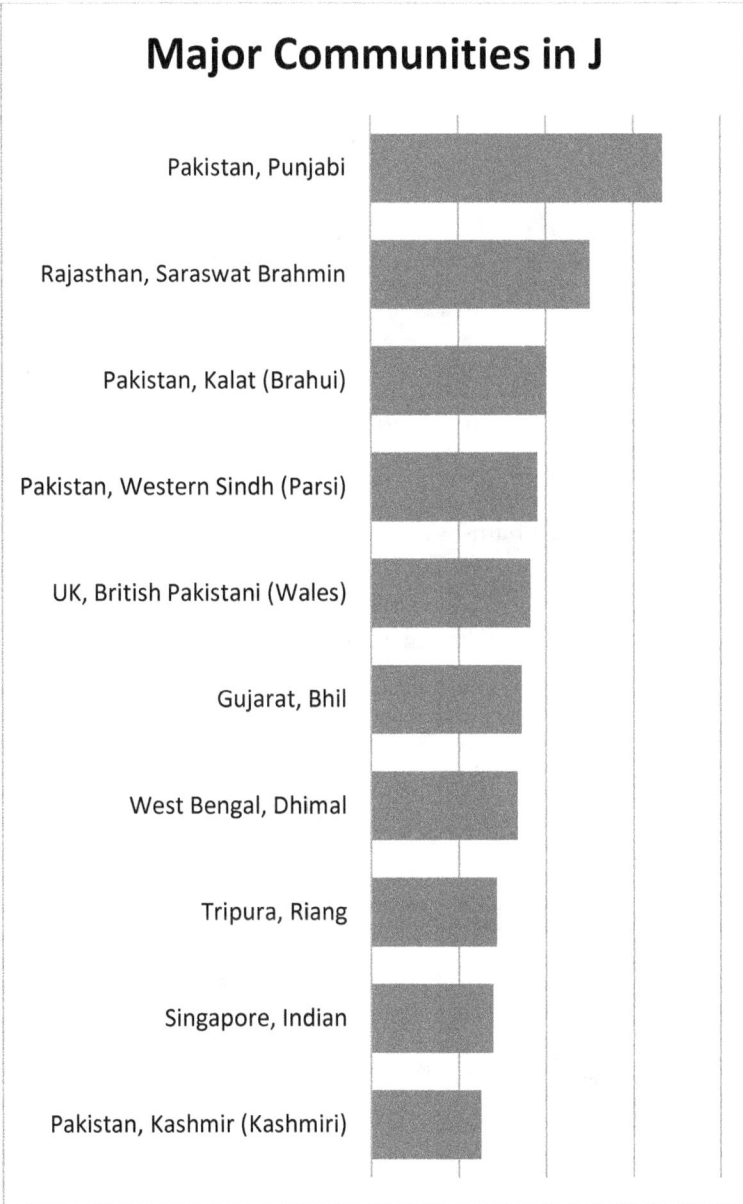

8.10 - Community Representation in J

David G. Mahal

HAPLOGROUP L

Ancestral Line on Phylogenetic Tree: M168 → M89 → M9 → M20 → M11

The ancestors of this group arrived in India twenty-five to thirty thousand years ago. This group is part of the Eurasian clan that migrated south once it reached the mountainous Pamir Knot region (Hindu Kush, the Tian Shan, and the Himalayas) in Tajikistan. The group and its subclades are found primarily in India, Pakistan, Afghanistan, Tajikistan, and Uzbekistan. It is found in low frequencies in the Middle East, parts of the Caucasus, and a few European countries. The group may be one of the creators of the Indus Valley Civilization.[4]

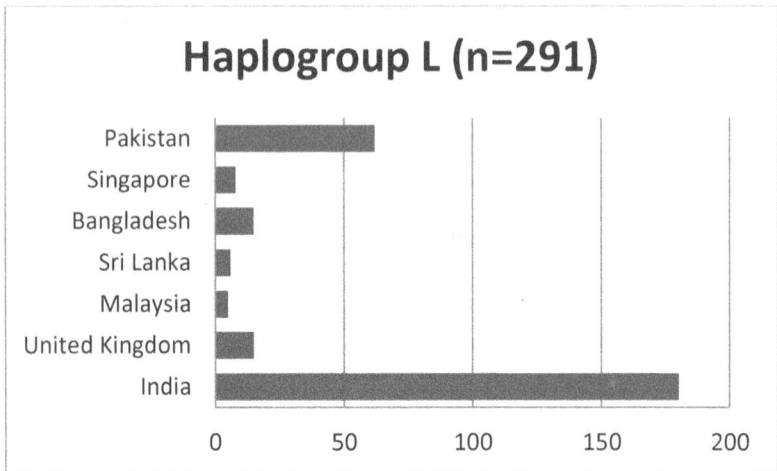

8.11 - Geographical Representation for L

164

Major Communities in L

West Bengal, Paliya

Tamil Nadu, Iyengar

Andhra Pradesh, Brahmin

West Bengal, Rajbanshi

Tamil Nadu, Kuruman

Maharashtra, Konkanastha Brahmin

Haryana, Jat

Punjab, Jat Sikh

Pakistan, Mastung (Baloch)

Bangladesh, Tangali (Garo)

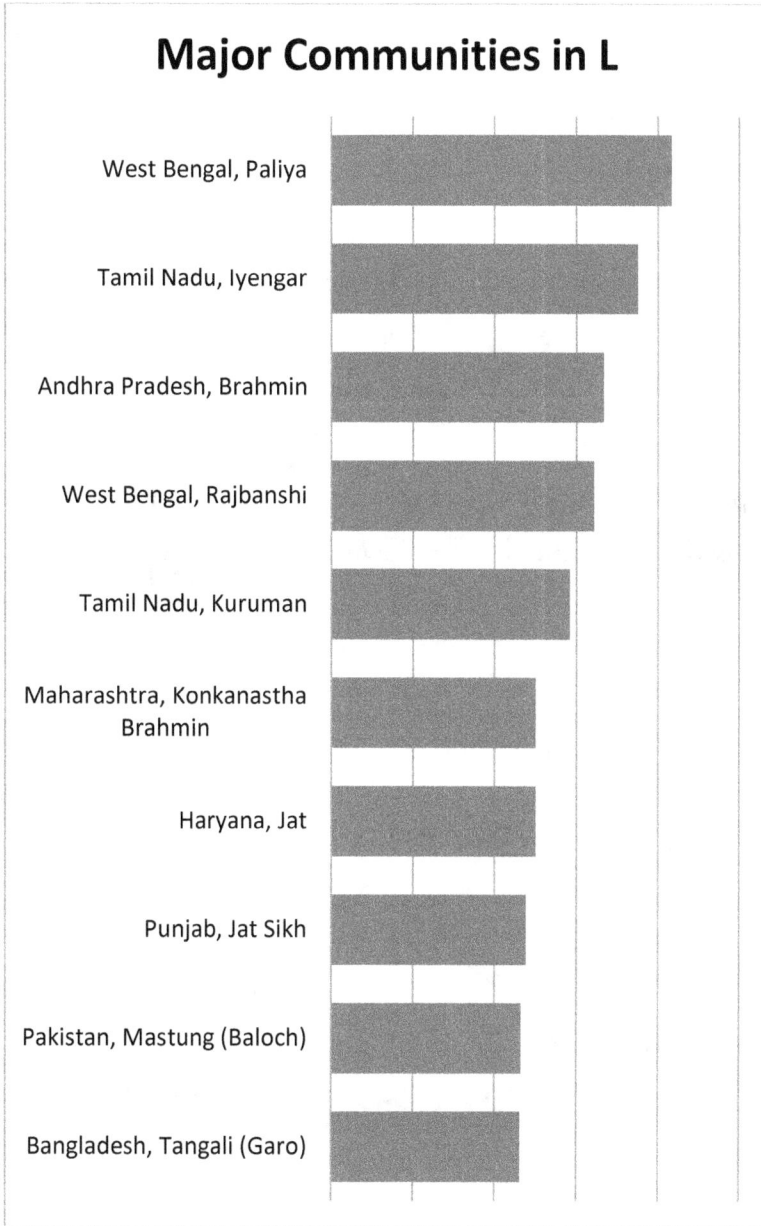

8.12 - Community Representation in L

David G. Mahal

HAPLOGROUP Q

Ancestral Line on Phylogenetic Tree: M168 → M89 → M9 → M45 → M242

The man with the M242 mutation was born in Siberia fifteen to twenty thousand years ago. His descendants traveled through northern Eurasia toward the east and crossed what was then the Beringia passage connecting Siberia and Alaska. They were the first people to reach North America.[5] Scientists have estimated that as few as twenty people may have founded the native population of the Americas.[6] Some members of the group moved to the western

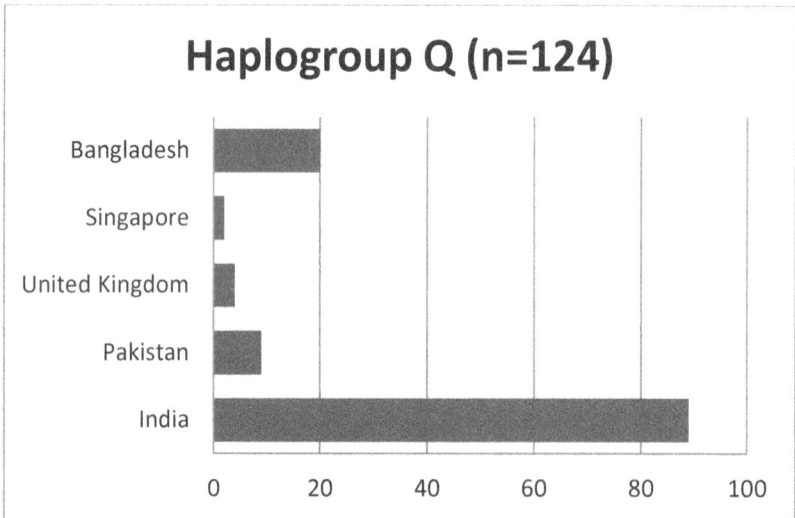

Haplogroup Q (n=124)

8.13 - Geographical Representation for Q

and southern areas. The descendants, known as the Siberian clan, are found in Siberia, China, and India. The group is also linked to the Huns, Mongols, and Turkic people.

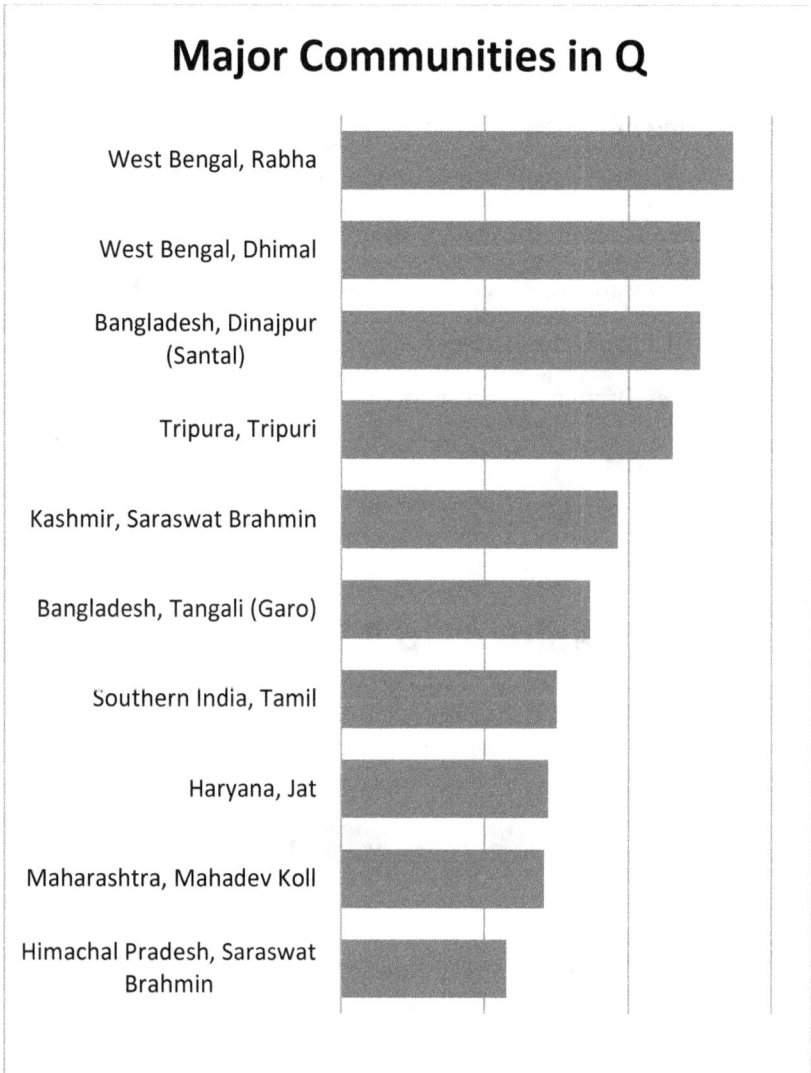

Major Communities in Q

West Bengal, Rabha
West Bengal, Dhimal
Bangladesh, Dinajpur (Santal)
Tripura, Tripuri
Kashmir, Saraswat Brahmin
Bangladesh, Tangali (Garo)
Southern India, Tamil
Haryana, Jat
Maharashtra, Mahadev Koll
Himachal Pradesh, Saraswat Brahmin

8.14 - Community Representation in Q

David G. Mahal

HAPLOGROUP R

Ancestral Line on Phylogenetic Tree: M168 → M89 → M9 → M45 → M207

After arriving in central Asia, the descendants of the man carrying the M207 mutation split into two groups. One group went west toward Europe, and the other headed south to arrive in India about ten thousand years ago. Branches of this group are found in all parts of Europe, the British Isles, and the Americas after recent migrations. A branch of these people is believed to be the first speakers of the Indo-European languages and responsible for the domestication of the horse around 3000 BCE.

Haplogroup R (n=276)

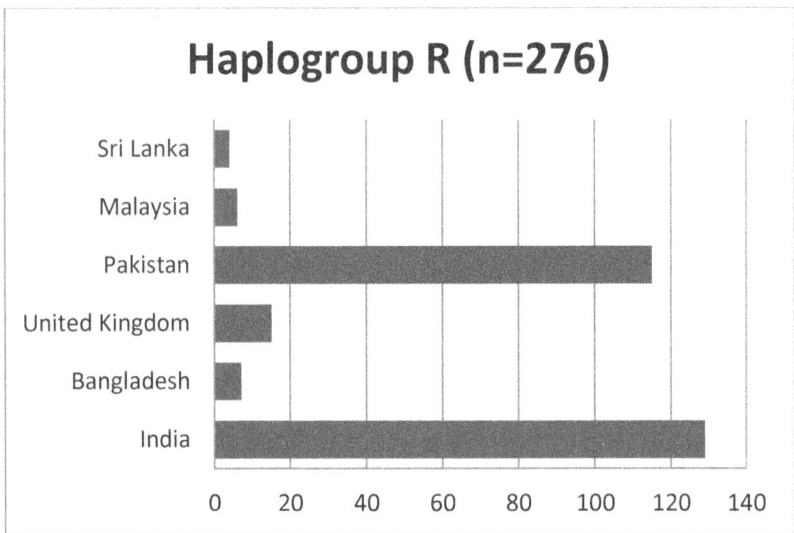

8.15 - Geographical Representation for R

The Khyber Pakhtunkhwa (Yousafzai Pathan) community in Pakistan has the highest representation in the sample. This is one of the largest haplogroups in India and Pakistan.

Major Communities in R

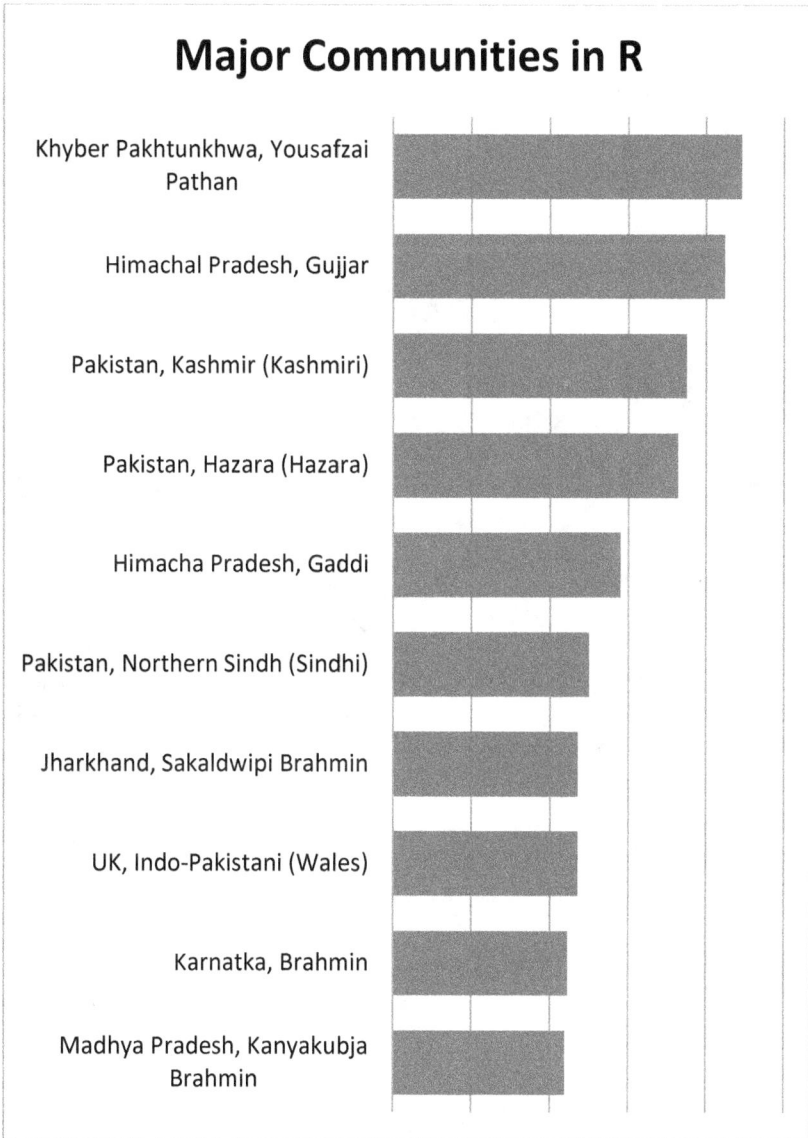

- Khyber Pakhtunkhwa, Yousafzai Pathan
- Himachal Pradesh, Gujjar
- Pakistan, Kashmir (Kashmiri)
- Pakistan, Hazara (Hazara)
- Himacha Pradesh, Gaddi
- Pakistan, Northern Sindh (Sindhi)
- Jharkhand, Sakaldwipi Brahmin
- UK, Indo-Pakistani (Wales)
- Karnatka, Brahmin
- Madhya Pradesh, Kanyakubja Brahmin

8.16 - Community Representation in R

David G. Mahal

HAPLOGROUP ORIGINS

The approximate geographical origins of the haplogroups are shown in the following map. The haplogroups C, O, N and T, which were not covered in detail in the study because of low representation, are included. The origins of three key markers for the ancestors of these haplogroups are also shown (see phylogenetic tree in chapter 6).

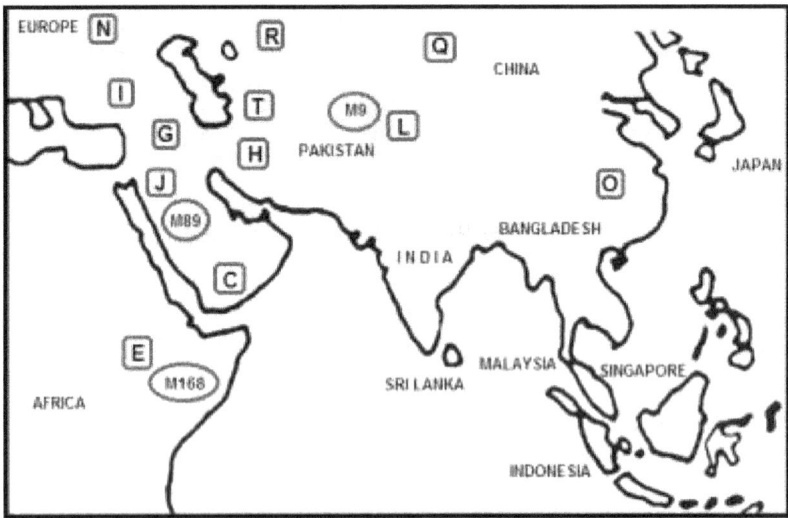

8.17 - Origins of Haplogroups

CHAPTER 9

CONCLUSION

"It is the traveler from an antique land who lives within us all."—Bryan Sykes

The states of Punjab in the north and Kerala in the south are located in the opposite corners of India and separated by about 1,500 miles (2,400 kilometers). The communities of Jat Sikhs from Punjab and the Ezhavas from Kerala have distinctly different cultures in terms of language, religion, cuisine, and history. In 2010, a study of the paternal lineage of the Ezhava community was conducted at the Sree Buddha College of Engineering in Kerala. It revealed that of the 104 haplotypes tested, ten were identical to the Jat Sikh population and four to the Turkish population. Based on the genotype, the Ezhavas showed more resemblance to Jat Sikh and Turkish populations than to East Asians.[1]

Other remarkable linkages appear among the different communities. Even with the traditional endogamous practices of people in the subcontinent, who generally marry within their own castes and communities, it cannot be said that their genes

David G. Mahal

have remained relatively pure over time. Perhaps endogamy was not as prevalent in the distant past when the populations were much smaller.

Vincent Smith was an Irish-born Indologist and historian who lived and worked in India between 1871 and 1900 as an officer in the Indian Civil Service. He wrote several books about the country, and said the following about the people of India:

> "In my judgment it is absolutely impossible to decide who were the earliest inhabitants of India, either in the north or the south, or to ascertain whence they came. Nor can we say what their bodily type was. The modern population of India almost everywhere is far too mixed ... The mixture of races on Indian soil was going on for countless ages before any history was recorded, and it is hopeless now to unravel the different lines of descent."[2]

About 100 years later, DNA science can unravel the ancestral lines of descent. But the population of the subcontinent is indeed very mixed. After seeing the results of many research studies, Dr. Ramasamy Pitchappan, head of National Geographic's Genographic Project in India, also says that "no caste is 'pure.'"

As we have seen earlier, people from the subcontinent belong to several different haplogroups or ancestral lines. Each haplogroup has its own distinct ancestor who came to the subcontinent long ago and started a family that flourished and dispersed in different directions. Eight major haplogroups—E, G, H, I, J, L, Q, and R—were identified and described. There is no major ethnic community in our study that can genetically trace the ancestry of its entire people to any single ancestor or race.

The following chart 9.1 shows all people in our study from India, Pakistan, and some adjoining countries, who belong to the eight haplogroups. Even with their different languages, religions, nationalities, customs, cuisines, and physical appearances, the people in the same haplogroup have a common ancestor in the distant past. The chart reflects the genetic links of these people. We need to keep in mind that Pakistan, Bangla Desh, Sri Lanka, and even Myanmar (Burma), were a part of India at one time.

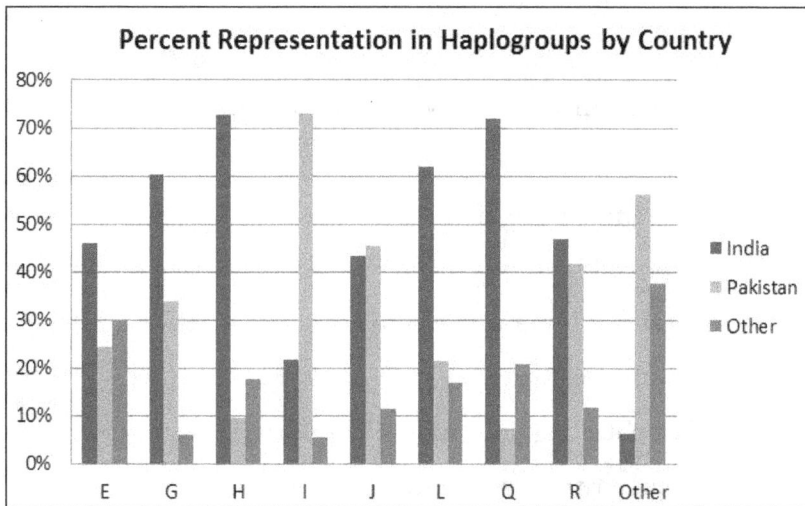

9.1 - People in the same haplogroups

David G. Mahal

WHAT IS YOUR HAPLOGROUP?

So where did your ancestors come from? Was it Africa, the Middle East, Europe, Central Asia, Siberia, or somewhere else? If this book has sparked an interest in determining your ancestral roots, what steps you can take? Here are some suggestions:

1. Have your DNA analyzed. This is a simple, painless test (a sample of saliva is all that is usually needed) that can be performed through a number of laboratories in the United States and Europe, some of which are named in the Resources section. We could not locate any laboratories on the Indian subcontinent that perform such tests for individuals at this time (apparently these laboratories test mostly for forensic, medical and research purposes). Hence, they are not included in the list.

2. The test can be performed for both the paternal (Y-DNA) and maternal (MT-DNA) sides for males and for the maternal side only for females. Females who are interested in determining their paternal ancestry can have the test performed by a close male relative. Depending on the type of test used, the results should provide both a haplotype and a haplogroup.

3. After obtaining your results, consider joining one or more of the surname and lineage projects at websites such as Ancestry.com and FamilyTreeDNA.com (see Resources section).

4. Consider creating your family tree and storing it on a website or in a software program. Younger members of your family can update and carry this information forward in time in a digital format that will last for a long time.

LOOKING AHEAD

The human population and the gene pool continue to expand. About 200,000 babies are added to this planet every day. That means there are about 140 new mouths to feed and deal with per minute. About nine billion people are expected to inhabit Earth by 2050. India is projected to become the most populated country on this planet by 2030. It will also have the largest pool of human genes. With the continuous movements and migrations of people to different parts of the world, their genes will continue to disperse around the globe.

As is often the case with science, the model of genealogy and genetic analysis is constantly evolving. The information provided in this book is based on current scientific evidence and understanding. This knowledge base will certainly continue to advance in the years to come.

Appendix

Ethnic Data

"To forget one's ancestors is to be a brook without
a source, a tree without a root."
— Chinese proverb

The following charts show the percentage distribution in haplogroups for the fifty two ethnic communities in the study. The major haplogroups for each community are identified in the left column (see chapter 8 for their descriptions). In some cases, because of a small sample size (n), the data may not necessarily reflect the true distribution for the community's total population, but they serve as indicators.

India, Andhra Pradesh, Brahmin
n = 12

E	17%
L	67%
R	17%
Total	100%

INDIA, GUJARAT, BHIL
n = 35

G	20%
H	11%
I	9%
J	34%
L	14%
Q	9%
R	3%
Total	100%

INDIA, HARYANA, JAT
n = 52

G	4%
J	13%
L	50%
Q	29%
R	4%
Total	100%

INDIA, HIMACHAL PRADESH, SARASWAT BRAHMIN
n = 13

J	8%
L	31%
Q	23%
R	38%
Total	100%

David G. Mahal

INDIA, HIMACHAL PRADESH, GUJJAR
n = 39

H	10%
J	5%
R	85%
Total	100%

INDIA, HIMACHAL PRADESH, GADDI
n = 19

G	11%
H	21%
J	11%
R	58%
Total	100%

INDIA, JHARKHAND, SAKALDWIPI BRAHMIN
n = 17

C	12%
H	41%
R	47%
Total	100%

INDIA, JHARKHAND, MUNDA
n = 25

H	16%
I	12%
O	72%
Total	100%

INDIA, JAMMU, SARASWAT BRAHMIN
n = 21

H	5%
J	10%
L	43%
Q	10%
R	33%
Total	100%

INDIA, KARNATKA, BRAHMIN
n = 18

E	6%
I	11%
J	11%
L	17%
Q	11%
R	44%
Total	100%

INDIA, KASHMIR, SARASWAT BRAHMIN
n = 13

H	8%
J	15%
L	38%
Q	38%
Total	100%

INDIA, MADHYA PRADESH, KANYAKUBJA BRAHMIN
n = 16

G	19%
H	13%
J	19%
Q	6%
R	44%
Total	100%

INDIA, MADHYA PRADESH, GOND
n = 23

G	9%
H	61%
L	17%
R	13%
Total	100%

INDIA, MAHARASHTRA, KONKANASTHA BRAHMIN
n = 14

E	14%
J	7%
L	50%
Q	7%
R	21%
Total	100%

INDIA, MAHARASHTRA, MAHADEV KOLL
n = 46

E	13%
H	24%
I	15%
J	7%
L	13%
Q	28%
Total	100%

INDIA, PUNJAB, SARASWAT BRAHMIN
n = 14

H	7%
J	7%
L	29%
Q	29%
R	29%
Total	100%

INDIA, PUNJAB, JAT SIKH
n = 42

E	5%
J	12%
L	48%
Q	5%
R	31%
Total	100%

David G. Mahal

INDIA, PUNJAB, BALMIKI
n = 36

H	75%
J	11%
L	3%
Q	11%
Total	100%

INDIA, RAJASTHAN, SARASWAT BRAHMIN
n = 28

H	11%
J	50%
L	14%
R	25%
Total	100%

INDIA, SOUTHERN INDIA, TAMIL
n = 20

E	15%
G	5%
H	5%
J	5%
L	40%
Q	30%
Total	100%

INDIA, TAMIL NADU, IYENGAR
n = 12

J	17%
L	75%
M	8%
Total	100%

182

INDIA, TAMIL NADU, KURUMAN
n = 24

H	17%
I	8%
J	4%
L	58%
Q	13%
Total	100%

INDIA, TRIPURA, RIANG
n = 21

H	14%
J	29%
L	29%
Q	19%
R	10%
Total	100%

INDIA, TRIPURA, TRIPURI
n = 13

J	23%
L	31%
Q	46%
Total	100%

INDIA, UTTAR PRADESH, AFRIDI PATHAN
n = 55

E	2%
G	60%
I	11%
J	9%
L	7%
R	11%
Total	100%

David G. Mahal

INDIA, WEST BENGAL, DHIMAL
n = 18

I	6%
J	33%
L	11%
Q	50%
Total	100%

INDIA, WEST BENGAL, PALIYA
n = 18

J	6%
L	83%
R	11%
Total	100%

INDIA, WEST BENGAL, RABHA
n = 11

L	27%
Q	55%
R	18%
Total	100%

INDIA, WEST BENGAL, RAJBANSHI
n = 14

J	14%
L	64%
Q	7%
R	14%
Total	100%

BANGLADESH, BANGLADESHI

n = 16

H	25%
J	13%
L	19%
Q	6%
R	38%
Total	100%

BANGLADESH, DINAJPUR (SANTAL)

n = 20

H	30%
I	10%
Q	50%
T	10%
Total	100%

BANGLADESH, TANGALI (GARO)

n = 26

J	12%
L	46%
Q	35%
T	8%
Total	100%

MALAYSIA, INDIAN

n = 27

E	19%
G	4%
H	15%
J	22%
L	19%
R	22%
Total	100%

PAKISTAN, BALTISTAN (BALTI)
n = 11

I	18%
J	18%
R	36%
T	27%
Total	100%

PAKISTAN, CHITRAL (KALASH)
n = 32

G	19%
H	16%
I	16%
J	19%
L	25%
N	6%
Total	100%

PAKISTAN, HAZARA (HAZARA)
n = 22

I	9%
N	5%
Q	9%
R	73%
T	5%
Total	100%

PAKISTAN, HUNZA (BURUSHO)
n = 49

H	10%
I	22%
J	14%
L	27%
Q	10%
R	16%
Total	100%

PAKISTAN, KALAT (BRAHUI)
n = 45

G	42%
I	9%
J	40%
R	9%
Total	100%

PAKISTAN, KASHMIR (KASHMIRI)
n = 12

J	25%
R	75%
Total	100%

PAKISTAN, KHYBER PAKHTUNKHWA (PATHAN)
n = 36

J	6%
L	6%
R	89%
Total	100%

David G. Mahal

PAKISTAN, MAKRAN COAST (BALOCH)
n = 12

E	8%
G	8%
I	33%
J	25%
L	17%
R	8%
Total	100%

PAKISTAN, MAKRAN COAST (NEGROID)
n = 15

E	13%
H	13%
I	20%
J	13%
Q	13%
R	27%
Total	100%

PAKISTAN, MASTUNG (BALOCH)
n = 28

E	7%
I	18%
J	7%
L	46%
R	21%
Total	100%

PAKISTAN, NORTHERN SINDH (SINDHI)
n = 36

I	14%
J	17%
L	14%
N	6%
R	50%
Total	100%

PAKISTAN, PATHAN
n = 41

E	5%
I	61%
L	15%
R	15%
T	5%
Total	100%

PAKISTAN, PUNJABI
n = 33

E	6%
G	6%
J	67%
L	6%
R	15%
Total	100%

David G. Mahal

PAKISTAN, WESTERN SINDH (PARSI)
n = 50

I	30%
J	38%
L	22%
R	4%
T	6%
Total	100%

SINGAPORE, INDIAN
n = 18

E	6%
I	6%
J	28%
L	44%
Q	11%
R	6%
Total	100%

SRI LANKA, SRI LANKAN
n = 20

E	10%
G	20%
H	10%
L	30%
R	20%
T	10%
Total	100%

United Kingdom, British Pakistani (Wales)
n = 11

E	18%
H	9%
J	36%
L	27%
Q	9%
Total	100%

United Kingdom, Indo-Pakistani (London)
n = 25

E	4%
H	12%
I	12%
J	12%
L	20%
Q	12%
R	28%
Total	100%

United Kingdom, Indo-Pakistani (Wales)
n = 17

H	12%
L	41%
R	47%
Total	100%

GLOSSARY

ALLELE: A variant form of a gene at a particular locus (location) on a chromosome. It represents the number of repeats in a STR marker (see *short tandem repeats*).

ARCHAEOLOGY: The study of material remains of past human life.

ANTHROPOLOGY: The study of humans, their origins, classification, and relationship of races.

BASE PAIR: The two bases that form the ladder of the DNA molecule. The bases are the letters that spell out the genetic code. The letters are A (Adenine), T (Thymine), G (Guinine), and C (Cytosine). A always pairs with T, and G always pairs with C.

BCE: Before the Current Era (same as BC).

CE: Of the Common Era (same as AD).

CELL: The smallest independent unit of living matter.

CHROMOSOMES: The long, threadlike strands of DNA on which genes are found.

CLADE AND SUBCLADE: A subhaplogroup.

CONSANGUINITY: A "shared blood" relationship.

CUNEIFORM: The written language that was invented in Mesopotamia (in Sumer, present Iraq) around 3,200 BCE.

DENISOVANS: The group of prehumans that left Africa three hundred to four hundred thousand years ago and ventured east toward Asia.

DEOXYRIBONUCLEIC ACID (DNA): The molecule inside the nucleus of a cell that carries the organism's genetic information.

DYS NUMBER: The genetic markers on the Y chromosome. D stands for DNA, Y for Y chromosome, and S for a unique segment of DNA.

DOUBLE HELIX: The shape of DNA that resembles a spiral staircase or twisted ladder.

GENE: The segment of DNA that is the basic unit of heredity and is passed from parent to offspring.

GENEALOGY: Tracing human lineage through DNA testing and comparison of haplotypes.

GENETICS: The science of genes, heredity, and variation in living organisms.

HAPLOGROUP: A population group descended from a common ancestor based on SNP mutations (see *single nucleotide polymorphism*). The haplogroups are assigned alphanumeric labels that can be shown on a phylogenetic or haplogroup tree. It is like the branch on a tree.

HAPLOTYPE: The set of results obtained from multiple markers located on a single chromosome. It is like the leaf on a branch.

HOMO ERECTUS: Prehumans that walked erect, were well established by about five hundred thousand years ago, and lived in various parts of the world.

David G. Mahal

HOMO HABILIS: Prehumans that lived from 1.4 to 2.4 million years ago.

HOMO HEIDELBERGENIS: Prehumans that evolved from *Homo erectus* and lived from two hundred thousand to one million years ago in various parts of Asia, Africa, and Europe.

HOMO SAPIENS: The modern human.

LOCUS: A location on a chromosome identified by a marker.

MARKER: An identifiable physical location on a chromosome that varies between individuals. It is used with allele values to describe an individual's haplotype.

MITOCHONDRIAL EVE: The most recent common female ancestor of all humans.

MOST RECENT COMMON ANCESTOR (MRCA): The shared ancestor of two or more people who represents their most recent link.

MT-DNA: Genetic material passed from mothers to their children, but only females are able to pass it on.

MUTATION: A permanent structural alteration in DNA.

NEANDERTHAL: The group of prehumans that left Africa three hundred to four hundred thousand years ago and ventured northwest into West Asia and Europe.

NUCLEOTIDE: A DNA building block that contains a base or half of a staircase step on the double helix.

PALEONTOLOGY: The study of what fossils tell us about the past and about our evolution as humans.

PHYLOGENY: Shown as a tree that illustrates the relations and development of all species.

REPLICATION: The process by which two DNA strands separate and create a new strand. During reproduction, the double helix unwinds and duplicates itself to pass on genetic information to the next generation.

SINGLE NUCLEOTIDE POLYMORPHISM (SNP): Small changes that create a person's unique DNA pattern.

SHORT TANDEM REPEAT (STR): The patterns in the DNA sequence that repeat. The allele values in the haplotype represent the number of repeats.

Y-ADAM: The most recent common male ancestor of all humans.

Y-DNA: Genetic material passed from fathers to sons essentially unaltered except for occasional mutations.

X AND Y CHROMOSOMES: The chromosomes that determine sex. Females have two X chromosomes, and males have one X and one Y chromosome.

ACKNOWLEDGMENTS

I am indebted to the National Geographic Society for instigating my interest in genetics and genealogy. In particular, the books and articles written by Dr. Spencer Wells, director of the Genographic Project at National Geographic Society, and Dr. Luigi Cavalli-Sforza at Stanford University, inspired me to dig further and learn about our past and ancestors. I started bewildered and—thanks to these gentlemen—ended enlightened.

Remembering the adage "A picture is worth a thousand words," I have used several pictures, maps, charts, and graphs. Unless stated otherwise, the maps and photographs are in the public domain and used courtesy of Wikimedia Commons. The charts and graphs were created in-house.

The illustrations of the Wilkinson Microwave Anisotropy Probe (WMAP) and Rosetta satellites in chapter 2 are used courtesy of the US National Aeronautics and Space Administration (NASA). In the same chapter, the image of the 67P Churyumov-Gerasimenko comet ("Chury") is used courtesy of the European Space Agency (ESA).

The map depicting migrations out of Africa in chapter 3 was proposed by Dr. Naruya Saitou at the (Japanese) National Institute for Genetics, and it originally appeared on the Kyushu Museum website in Japan.

Dr. Alan Bittles of the Centre for Comparative Genomics at Murdoch University, Australia, kindly allowed me to use the map of Consanguineous Marriages Worldwide in chapter 5.

The illustration of the human cell in chapter 6 is used with the permission of FamilyTreeDNA.com. In the same chapter, the illustrations of chromosomes, the double helix, and the human gene are used courtesy of the US National Library of Medicine.

The data maintained by YHRD.org was invaluable in conducting my research about Indian haplogroups. Whit Athey's Haplogroup Predictor made the job easier.

The definitions of haplogroups are summarized from Charles Kerchner's website http://www.kerchner.com/haplogroups-ydna.htm, the website "Y Haplogroups" at Nechbet.com, and the book *Deep Ancestry* by Spencer Wells.

NOTES

PREFACE

1. Alex Haley, *Roots: The Saga of an American Family* (New York: Doubleday, 1976).

2. Max Fischer, "DNA tests estimate that Prince William is 0.3 to 0.8 percent Indian," *Washington Post,* June 14, 2013.

3. Ujagar Singh Mahil, *Antiquity of Jat Race* (New Delhi: Atma Ram & Sons, 1955).

4. The Genographic Project, National Geographic Society, https://genographic.nationalgeographic.com.

CHAPTER 1: CREATING HISTORY

1. Dan Brown, *The Da Vinci Code* (New York: Anchor, 2009).

2. "Attila," Wikipedia, http://en.wikipedia.org/wiki/Attila

3. Hector Munro Chadwick, *The Heroic Age* (Cambridge: Cambridge University Press, 1926).

4. "Herodotus," Ancient History Encyclopedia, http://www.ancient.eu/herodotus/

5. Plutarch, Lionel Pearson (translator), *Moralia XI, On the Malice of Herodotuss,* (Cambridge, MA: Harvard University Press (Loeb Classical Library), 1965).

6. "Herodotus," *Wikipedia,* http://en.wikipedia.org/wiki/Herodotus.

7. Alan Fildes and Joann Fletcher, *Alexander the Great: Son of the Gods* (Los Angeles: Getty Publications, 2002).

8. Vincent A. Smith, *The Oxford History of India* (London: Oxford University Press, 1919).

9. Sir Herbert Hope Risely, *Imperial Gazetteer of India*, (London: Oxford at the Clarendon Press, 1909).

10. Herodotus, Aubrey de Selincourt (translator), The *Histories* (London: Penguin Books, 1954).

11. Paul Raffaele, "Sleeping with Cannibals," *Smithsonian*, September 2006.

12. Michel Peissel. *The Ant's Gold: The Discovery of the Greek El Dorado in the Himalayas* (Hammersmith, UK: HarperCollins, 1984).

13. "Takshila: World's first University," *Incredible India*, February 26, 2009, http://incredibleindia.blogspot.com.

14. "Thucydides," History.com, http://www.history.com/topics/thucydides.

15. Vinay Kumar, *Social Life in Ancient India as Described in the Indika of Ktesias* (Pune, India: Bhandarkar Oriental Research Institute, 1974).

16. Ctesias, *Ancient India as Described by Ktesias the Knidian*, translation from *Indika* (RareBooksClub.com, 2012).

17. H. H. Wilson, *Notes on the Indica of Ctesias* (Oxford: The Ashmolean Society, 1836).

18. A. V. Williams Jackson, "History of India," http://www.ibiblio.org.

19. Napoleon Bonaparte, The Quotations Page, http://www.quotationspage.com/quote/297.html

20. Martha Congleton Howell and Walter Prevenier, *Reliable Sources: An Introduction to Historical Methods* (Ithaca, NY: Cornell University Press, 2001).

Chapter 2: The Beginnings

1. Jessica Ravitz, "Indian Awakenings," CNN, June 2014, http://www.cnn.com/interactive/2014/06/world/rishikes.

2. Stephen Hawking and Leonard Mlodinow, *The Grand Design* (New York: Bantam Books, 2010).

3. "Wilkinson Microwave Anisotropy Probe," National Aeronautics and Space Administration, http://map.gsfc.nasa.gov.

4. "Attainment of Salvation," The Bhagavad Gita, http://www.bhagavad-gita.org/Gita/verse-08-17.html.

5. "Jainism" Religionfacts.com, http://www.religionfacts.com/jainism/index.htm.

6. Elizabeth Landau, "4.4 Billion-Year-Old Crystal Is Oldest Piece of Earth," CNN.com, http://www.cnn.com/2014/02/24/world/oldest-earth-fragment/index.html?hpt=hp_t2.

7. Will Dunham, "Oldest Rocks on Earth Found in Northern Canada," Reuters, http://www.reuters.com/article/2008/09/25/us-rocks-ancientscience.

8. Paul S. Braterman, "How Science Figured Out the Age of Earth," *Scientific American*, October 20, 2013.

9. Michael Eyre, "Complex organic molecule found in interstellar space," BBC, September 26, 2014, http://www.bbc.com/news/science-environment-29368984

10. John Gribbin, *The Universe: A Biography* (London: Penguin Books, 2008).

11. "The Earth Forms," BBC, http://www.bbc.co.uk/science/earth/earth_timeline/earth_formed

12. Nathaniel Rich, "Can a Jellyfish Unlock the Secret of Immortality?," The New York Times Magazine, November 22, 2012, http://www.nytimes.com/2012/12/02/magazine/can-a-jellyfish-unlock-the-secret-of-immortality.html?pagewanted=all&_r=0

13. Jim Bell, "Why Rosetta spacecraft chased after a comet," CNN Opinion, August 8, 2014, http://www.cnn.com/2014/08/08/opinion/bell-rosetta-comet/index.html?hpt=hp_t3

CHAPTER 3: HUMAN ORIGINS

1. Kristen Butler, "Oldest-Known Fossil Primate Skeleton Unearthed in China," *Science News,* http://www.upi.com/Science_News/2013/06/05.

2. Roger Highfield, "Scientists Unearth Six Million-Year-Old Remains in Africa," *Telegraph,* http://www.telegraph.co.uk.

3. "Lucy's Story," Institute of Human Origins, Arizona State University, https://iho.asu.edu/about/lucy%E2%80%99s-story.

4. Jeffrey Brown, "1.8 Million-Year-Old Skull May Revise Understanding of Human Evolution," Public Broadcasting Service, http://www.pbs.org.

5. C. Stories, "Oldest Human Fossil in Western Europe Found in Spain," *Popular Archaeology,* http://popular-archaeology.com.

6. K. A. Kennedy, A. Sonakia, J. Chiment, and K. K. Verma, "Is the Narmada Hominid an Indian Homo Erectus?" National Library of Medicine, http://www.ncbi.nlm.nih.gov/pubmed/1776655.

7. Parth R. Chauhan, "An Overview of the Siwalik Acheulian and Reconsidering Its Chronological Relationship with the Soanian–A Theoretical Perspective," *Assemblage,* http://www.assemblage.group.shef.ac.uk.

David G. Mahal

8. Carl Zimmer, "Interbreeding with Neanderthals," *Discover,* March 2013.

9. Michael Day, "Fossil Reanalysis Pushes Back Origin of Homo Sapiens," *Scientific American,* February 17, 2005.

10. Robert Sanders, "160,000-Year-Old fossilized skulls uncovered in Ethiopia are oldest anatomically modern humans," *UCBerkeleyNews,* June 11, 2003, http://www.berkeley.edu/news/media/releases/2003/06/11_oldest-humans.shtml

11. Luigi Luca Cavalli-Sforza et al., *The Great Human Diasporas: The History of Diversity and Evolution* (New York, NY: Perseus Books, 1996).

12. John Roach, "Massive Genetic Study Supports 'Out of Africa' Theory," *National Geographic News,* February 21, 2008.

13. Donald C. Johanson, "Origins of Modern Humans: Multiregional or Out of Africa?" American Institute of Biological Sciences, http://www.actionbioscience.org, May 2001.

14. David Whitehouse, "When Humans Faced Extinction," BBC News Online, http://news.bbc.co.uk/2/hi/science/nature/2975862.stm.

15. Tim Jones, "Mount Toba Eruption—Ancient Human Unscathed, Study Claims," http://www.antropology.net, July 2007.

16. Paul Hamaker, "Sri Lankan 'Balangoda Man' Dated to 37,000 Years Ago," Examiner.com, http://www.examiner.com/article/sri-lankan-balangoda-man-dated-to-37-000-years-ago.

17. Allen Worwood and Brittany Shamess, "The Great Human Migration," *Madurai Messenger,* July 2010.

18. Nina G. Jablonski, "Why Human Skin Comes in Colors," *AnthroNotes,* Spring 2011.

CHAPTER 4: MIGRATIONS AND WARFARE

1. William F. Fisher, *Toward Sustainable Development: Struggling over India's Narmada River* (Armonk, NY: M. E. Sharpe, 1995).

2. World Heritage Sites, "Rock Shelters of Bhimbetka," Archaeological Survey of India, http://asi.nic.in.

3. Nivedita Khandekar, "Indus Valley 2,000 Years Older Than Thought," *Hindustan Times,* November 4, 2012.

4. David R. Harris, *The Origins and Spread of Agriculture and Pastoralism in Eurasia* (New York: Routledge, 1996).

5. Gregory L. Possehl, *Oxford Companion to Archaeology, Mehrgarh* (Oxford: Oxford University Press, 1996).

6. "Mehrgarh Culture," Wikibooks.org, http://en.wikibooks.org/wiki/Ancient_History/Indian_subcontin ent/Mehrgarh_Culture.

7. A. Coppa et al., "Early Neolithic Tradition of Dentistry: Flint Tips Were Surprisingly Effective for Drilling Tooth Enamel in a Prehistoric Population," *Nature,* April 6, 2006.

8. Colin McEvedy and Richard Jones, *Atlas of World Population History* (New York, NY: Puffin-Penguin Books, 1978).

9. "Symbols Akin to Indus Valley Culture Discovered in Kerala," *The Hindu,* September 29, 2009.

10. Asko Parpola, "The Formation of the Aryan Branch of Indo-European," *World Archaeology: Archeaology and Language,* (London: Routledge, 1999).

11. Michael Wood, *India* (New York: Basic Books, 2007).

David G. Mahal

12. J. P. Mallory, *In Search of the Indo-Europeans: Language, Archaeology, and Myth* (London: Thames & Hudson, 1989).

13. Dinesh C. Sharma, "Indian Are Not Descendants of Aryans, Says New Study," *India Today*, December 2011.

14. "Armenians in India,"*Wikipedia*, http://en.wikipedia.org/wiki/Armenians_in_India.

15. Osmond Bopearachchi, "Monnaies Greco-Bactriennes et Indo-Grecques," *Wikepedia*, Bibliotheque Nationale, 1991, http://en.wikipedia.org/wiki/Osmund_Bopearachchi

16. Krishna Chandra Sagar, *Foreign Influence on Ancient India,* (New Delhi: Northern Book Centre, 1992).

17. M. Raja, "India's Ancient Spice Trade Gets a Makeover," *Asia Times*, September 18, 2007.

18. Stephen Neill, *A History of Christianity in India: The Beginning to AD 1707* (Cambridge: Cambridge University Press, 2004).

19. "The White Huns—The Hephthalites," The Silkroad Foundation, Saratoga, California, http://www.silkroad.com/artl/heph.shtml.

20. Hillary Mayell, "Genghis Khan a Prolific Lover, DNA Data Implies," *National Geographic News*, February 14, 2003.

21. Shiv Kumar Gupta, "Modernisation of the Army," *Sunday Tribune*, April 8, 2001, http://www.tribuneindia.com.

22. B. S. Ahloowalia, *Invasion of the Genes: Genetic Heritage of India* (New York: Eloquent Books, 2009).

CHAPTER 5: COUNTING RELATIVES

1. Brian Pears, "Our Ancestors, Conceptions, Misconceptions and a Paradox," bpears.org, http://www.bpears.org.uk.

2. Alan Boyle, "All Europeans Are Related If You Go Back Just 1,000 Years, Scientists Say," NBC News, May 7, 2013, http://cosmiclog.nbcnews.com/_news/2013/05/07/18107175-all-europeans-are-related-if-you-go-back-just-1000-years-scientists-say?lite.

3. Dan Vergano, "Ancient Incest Uncovered in Neanderthal Genome," *National Geographic Daily News*, December 18, 2013.

4. Russell Middleton, "Brother-Sister and Father-Daughter Marriage in Ancient Egypt," *American Sociological Review* 5, no. 27 (1962).

5. Trevor Bryce, *The Great Empires of the Ancient World* (Los Angeles: Getty Publications, 2009).

6. "Endogomy in the British Monarchy," *Wikipedia*, http://en.wikipedia.org/wiki/Endogomy_in_the_British_monarchy.

7. A. H. Bittles and M. L. Black, "Consanguineous Marriage and Human Evolution," *Annual Review of Anthropology* 39 (2010).

8. "Cousin Marriage in Islam," *WikiIslam*, http://wikiislam.net/wiki/Cousin_Marriage_in_Islam.

9. "Arabs Question Centuries-Old Tradition of Cousin Marriages," *Dawn Newspaper*, April 4, 2012, http://www.dawn.com.

10. Samira Shackle, "Professor Sparks 'Muslim Outrage.' Or Does He?" Yanabi.com, May 30, 2011, http://www.yanabi.com/index.php?/topic/421513-professor-sparks-muslim-outrage-or-does-he.

11. John Rowlatt, "The Risks of Cousin Marriage," BBC Newsnight, November 16, 2005, http://news.bbc.co.uk/2/hi/programmes/newsnight/4442010.stm.

David G. Mahal

12. Anne-Marie Nybo Andersen, "Flere dødfødsler blandt indvandrere," Jyllands-posten.dk, February 27, 2009, http://jyllands-posten.dk/livsstil/sundhed/ECE4116348/flere-doedfoedsler-blandt-indvandrere.

13. Shrikant Kuntla, Srinivas Goli, P. Arokiasamy, "Revisiting Consanguineous Marriages and Their Effect on Pregnancy, Outcomes in India: Evidences from a Nation-wide Survey" (proceedings, Population Association of America annual meeting, San Francisco, 2012).

14. A. Alwan and B. Modell, "Community Control of Genetic and Congenital Disorders," WHO Regional Office Mediterranean Region, Egypt, *EMRO Technical Publication* 24 (1997).

15. Robert Conniff, "Go Ahead, Kiss Your Cousin," *Discover*, August, 2003.

16. B. Mallikarjun, "Mother Tongues of India According to the 1961 Census," LanguageinIndia.com, August 5, 2002, http://www.languageinindia.com/aug2002/indianmothertongues1961aug2002.html.

CHAPTER 6: GENES AND GENEALOGY

1. Gina Smith, *The Genomics Age: How DNA Technology is Transforming the Way We Live and Who We Are*, (New York: AMACOM, 2004).

2. "Pharmacogenomics Program," The Mayo Clinic, http://mayoresearch.mayo.edu/center-for-individualized-medicine/pharmacogenomics.asp.

3. Alan Boyle, "Scientists Say Otzi the Iceman Has Living Relatives, 5,300 Years Later," NBC.com, October 14, 2013, http://www.nbcnews.com/science/science-news/scientists-say-otzi-iceman-has-living-relatives-5-300-years-f8C11392771.

4. "DNA Wars: How the Cell Strikes Back to Avoid Disease after Attacks on DNA," MIT OpenCourseWare, Massachussetts Institute of Technology, http://ocw.mit.edu/courses/biology/7-346-dna-wars-how-the-cell-strikes-back-to-avoid-disease-after-attacks-on-dna-fall-2013/

5. Spencer Wells, *Deep Ancestry* (Washington, DC: National Geographic Society, 2007).

6. Megan Smolenyak Smolenyak and Ann Turner, *Trace Your Roots with DNA* (Emmaus, PA: Rodale Books, 2004).

CHAPTER 7: THE ANCESTORS

1. Spencer Wells, *The Journey of Man: A Genetic Odyssey* (Princeton, NJ: Princeton University Press, 2002).

CHAPTER 8: MAJOR HAPLOGROUPS

1. P. A. Underhill et al., "The Phylogeography of Y Chromosome Binary Haplotypes and the Origins of Modern Human Populations," *Annals of Human Genetics* 65 (2001).

2. D. Behar, "The Genome-Wide Structure of the Jewish People," *Nature*, July, 2010.

3. Charles Kerchner, "YDNA Haplogroup Descriptions and Information Links," Kerchner.com, http://www.kerchner.com/haplogroups-ydna.htm.

4. S. Sengupta et al., "Polarity and Temporality of High-Resolution Y-Chromosome Distributions in India Identify Both Indigenous and Exogenous Expansions and Reveal Minor Genetic Influence of Central Asian Pastoralists," *American Journal of Human Genetics* (2006), 202–221.

David G. Mahal

5. Alok Jha, "Human Arrived in North America 2,500 Years Earlier Than Thought," *Guardian,* March 24, 2011.

6. Dennis Liu, "Using DNA to Trace Human Migration," Howard Hughes Medical Institute, http://www.hhmi.org/biointeractive/using-dna-trace-human-migration.

Chapter 9: Conclusion

1. S.P. Nair, A. Geetha, and C. Jagannath, "Y-Short Tandem Repeat Haplotype and Paternal Lineage of the Ezhava Population of Kerala, South India," National Library of Medicine, June 2011, http://www.ncbi.nlm.nih.gov/pubmed/?term=Geetha+A.+Nair.

2. Vincent A. Smith, *The Oxford History of India from the Earliest Times to the End of 1911* (Oxford: Oxford University Press, 1928).

RESOURCES

SUGGESTED READING

Bryson, Bill. *A Short History of Nearly Everything*. New York: Broadway Books, 2003.

Cavalli-Sforza, Luigi Luca, and Francesco Cavalli-Sforza. *The Great Human Diasporas: The History of Diversity and Evolution*. Reading, MA: Perseus Books, 1995.

Coyne, Jerry A. *Why Evolution Is True*. New York, NY: Viking Penguin Books, 2009.

Fitzpatrick, Colleen and Andrew Yeiser. *DNA and Genealogy*. Fountain Valley, CA: Rice Book Press, 2005.

Gribbin, John. *The Universe: A Biography*. London: Penguin Books, 2008.

Smolenyak, Megan and Ann Turner. *Trace Your Roots with DNA: Using Genetic Tests to Explore Your Family Tree*. Emmanus, PA: Rodale Press, 2004.

Wells, Spencer. *The Journey of Man: A Genetic Odyssey*. Princeton, NJ: Princeton University Press, 2003.

Wood, Michael. *India*. New York: Basic Books, 2007.

DNA TESTING LABORATORIES

23andme, http://www.23andme.com

Ancestry.com, http://www.Ancestry.com

David G. Mahal

BritainsDNA, http://www.britainsdna.com

FamilyTreeDNA, http://www.familytreedna.com

GenTrace, http://www.dnafamilycheck.com

National Geographic Genographic Project,
https://genographic.nationalgeographic.com

Oxford Ancestors
http://www.oxfordancestors.com/component/option,com_front
page/Itemid,1

Note: Several laboratories in India, Pakistan, and Bangladesh
conduct DNA tests but mostly for forensic, medical, and research
purposes. Attempts were made to determine if they conduct such
tests for individuals but the responses were not affirmative. This
may change.

USEFUL WEBSITES

Howard Hughes Medical Institute,
http://www.hhmi.org/biointeractive/using-dna-trace-human-
migration

Institute of Human Origins, Arizona State University,
https://iho.asu.edu

National Geographic Genographic Project,
https://genographic.nationalgeographic.com

Smithsonian National Museum of History,
http://humanorigins.si.edu/research

INDEX

David G. Mahal

Homo erectus narmadensis,
51
Homo habilis, 49
Homo heidelbergensis, 52,
54
Homo sapiens balangodensis,
58
Human Genome Project, 6,
121, 124
Humayun, 101
Hun kings, 91

Ibn al-Shatir, 29
Il Gran Mogul, 103
Iltutmish, 96
Indian Ocean, 27, 28, 92, 100
Indika, 24, 96, 199
Indonesia, 50, 56, 58, 104
Indo-Pakistani, 191
Indo-Scythian, 85
Indus civilization, 19
Indus Valley, 18, 21, 22, 65,
67, 68, 69, 70, 71, 72, 74,
156, 164, 203
Iran, 67, 68, 70, 75, 93, 94,
158
Isaac Newton, 35
Islam, 92, 93, 97, 98, 101,
113, 205
iso-propyl cyanide, 40
Italian Alps, 156
Iyengar, 182

J. P. Mallory, 72
Jahangir, 101
Jainism, 22, 35, 39, 200
Jama Masjid, 102
Japanese occupation, 105
Jat Sikh, 171, 181

Jats, 4, 5, 152
Java Man, 50
Jean-François, 66
jellyfish, 40
Jesse Gelsinger, 123
Jet Propulsion Laboratory, 39
Jewish traders, 80
Johann Sebastian Bach, 116
John Adams, 115
John F. Fitzgerald, 116
Jwalapuram, 58

Kachi plain, 65
Kalash, 186
Kalinga War, 79
Kanishka, 89
Kanyakubja Brahmin, 180
Kashmiri, 151, 187
Kautalya, 80
Kerala, 69, 80, 89, 92, 100,
171, 203, 208
Ketavaram, 69
Khilji dynasty, 96
King Hussein of Jordan, 116
Kochi, 27
Konkanastha Brahmin, 180
Krishna River, 101
Kshatriya, 73
Ktesias, 14, 24, 96, 199
Kumarasamy Thangaraj, 74
Kuruman, 183
Kushans, 81, 87, 88, 91, 106

Lalji Singh, 74
language, 4, 7, 12, 13, 48, 56,
117, 171, 192
Life of Pi, 104
Lions, 21
locus, 133

ABOUT THE AUTHOR

David G. Mahal is the founder and president of DGM Associates, a business services and communications firm. Earlier, he held management positions at several multinational companies including Air India, Xerox Corporation, Hughes Helicopters, Tosco Corporation, and Atari Inc. His multifaceted career includes roles as a management consultant, software developer, instructor, author, and publisher.

David earned the advanced executive MBA degree from the Peter Drucker School of Management at Claremont Graduate University, the MS degree from the University of Rochester, and the BA degree from Dominican College. He is an instructor at the University of California, Los Angeles (UCLA).

David developed an interest in genetics and genealogy after having his DNA analyzed through the National Geographic Society's Genographic Project. Originally from India, he lives in Los Angeles.

www.ingramcontent.com/pod-product-compliance
Lightning Source LLC
Chambersburg PA
CBHW062052270326
41931CB00013B/3041